How To Become A Pokémon Master

How To Become A Pokémon Master

HANK SCHLESINGER

St. Martin's Paperbacks

HOW TO BECOME A POKÉMON MASTER

Copyright © 1999 by Hank Schlesinger.

ISBN: 0-312-97256-3

Printed in the United States of America

St. Martin's Paperbacks edition/August 1999

St. Martin's Paperbacks are published by St. Martin's Press, 175 Fifth Avenue, New York, N.Y. 10010.

10 9 8 7 6 5 4 3 2 1

This book is dedicated to
William Walker Schlesinger
and Maxwell Arthur
Schlesinger
and to
Melissa Suzanne, as always.

Contents

A Note To Parents
(Okay, okay, kids can read it too)

FOR MANY YOUNGSTERS, POKÉMON REPRE-
sents their first journey into the world of
video games. Pokémon represents a unique
phenomenon in the video game world. Not
only is it astoundingly popular, but it ap-
peals to both girls and boys of a young age.
For many of them, it is their first successful
video game experience and by no means
their last.

Video games are fun. There is no getting
around that fact. They are part of a kid's life
and one of the many entertainment choices
he or she has today. However, as the technology has improved over the years, games
have evolved in a fashion similar to movies.
Today video games include a wide variety
of themes, content, and situations. That is

to say, not all games are suitable for all age groups. Just as not all movies are suitable for young children because of violent or adult content, the same holds true for video games.

To their credit, video game manufacturers have acted as responsible adults in the matter. The Entertainment Software Rating Board (ESRB), whose formation was supported by the video game industry, independently rates all video games in much the same way as movies are rated. Indeed, as the available technology allows for ever more detailed screen representations, today's games move ever closer to movie-like action. For that reason, parents should regard selection of video games in the same cautious manner as movies.

It is a parent's responsibility—and the youngster's—to carefully monitor the types of video games that come into the home. Clearly displayed labeling listing the ratings on packages make this job easier. But it is up to the parent (and kid) to learn the rating symbols and what they mean.

Following is the ESRB's rating system.

E is for EVERYONE. E indicates that the game has content suitable for ages 6 or older. Older games may have a rating listed as K-A, which is identical.

T is for TEEN. T indicates that the game is suitable for kids 13 years and older.

M is for MATURE. M indicates that the game includes content that should be restricted to people 17 years or older.

A is for ADULTS ONLY. Should be played only by grown-ups.

RP is for RATING PENDING. The game has not yet received its final rating from the ESRB.

Of course, parents also should use their own good judgment regarding video games, just as they do with films and television shows. As an entertainment art form, video games have made unsurpassed technological progress over the past decade. With that progress has come a wider audience and wider range of games intended for young players. It is up to parents to restrict their child's play to age-appropriate video games.

All the games discussed in this book have been rated E by the ESRB. However, in the end, parental standards should be the final guidelines. The author of this book highly recommends that parents screen all video games for their children.

Does E Really Mean Everyone?

KIDS, THERE IS SOMETHING YOU SHOULD know. Just because a game is Rated E for Everyone doesn't mean that it is a "baby game." And it doesn't mean that *everyone* can play it really well. There are actually some "baby games" out there. For example, a game called Elmo's ABCs is a really good little-kids' game that teaches reading. It's probably too easy for you to play. You'd be bored. But there are also some very, very difficult games out there that are rated E. So you shouldn't get upset or feel bad if a game is too hard for you to play well. I hate to say "give up," but if you have tried really, really hard for a long time and just can't seem to get anywhere in the game, then maybe you should put it aside for a while and try another game. Remember, video games should be fun. So, if you aren't very good at sports games or having any fun with them, then try a role-playing game. If role-playing games aren't fun, then try a puzzle game.

There are hundreds of Game Boy games out there, so you are almost certain to find games you can play and enjoy.

How To Become A Pokémon Master

Introduction

I WAS SITTING IN MY FAVORITE CHAIR AND eating a bowl of my favorite cereal when the phone rang. It was some guy who said, "Know anything about Pokémon? Want to write a book about the game?"

I keep waiting for the phone to ring and some guy to say "Do you want to be a rock and roll star?" or "Do you want your own game show?" Those guys never call. A guy called once and asked me, "Are you happy with your long-distance company?" I told him I wasn't happy with my long-distance company, because my long-distance company came over once and ate all the strawberry out of the vanilla, strawberry, and chocolate ice cream. Another time my long-distance company squeezed the toothpaste from the middle of the tube. So I told him I was very unhappy with my long-distance company. But that's another story.

Now, I like Pokémon as well as the next guy. Okay, maybe a little more than the next guy. And if the next guy were here, I'd tell him that, right to his face. But writing a Pokémon book is hard work. For one thing, the game is so complicated and there is so much to do in the game that a book about Pokémon would have to be as thick as a dictionary—and not one of those pee-wee pocket dictionaries either. A book about Pokémon would have to be as thick as one of those giant-size dictionaries with all the giant-size words in it.

I wrote the book anyway. And yes, it was hard work, but it also was a lot of fun. I wrote the book to help kids have even more fun playing Pokémon. The book doesn't contain the entire game. There are hints and tricks and jokes you might like. There are also a bunch of forms you can fill out to keep track of stuff, such as what Pokémon you have caught or traded. I wrote the kind of book I'd like to read when I'm not playing the game.

I'll tell you why I like Pokémon. First off, I like the Game Boy. Always have and always will. The Game Boy is ten years old, probably as old as some of you guys reading this right now, maybe even older. For computer and video games, that's ancient. If your life were measured the same way as video games, you'd be old enough to be your own grandparent. You'd be wrinkly and talk about when you were a kid, seven years ago. *Those were the days.*

Fortunately, the Game Boy isn't wrinkly and doesn't tell stories about when it was a kid. It's still going strong. And that's due— at least in part—to Pokémon. Right now Pokémon is the best-selling Game Boy game. That says a lot about the Game Boy and a lot about Pokémon.

Now, if you bought (or had your parents buy) the Game Boy just for Pokémon, then you're making a big mistake. There are tons of very good games for the Game Boy, and you should try at least a few of them. Not trying some of the other games is like having a TV and watching only one show. Remember, no matter how much fun Pokémon is right now, sooner or later you are going to get bored with it. That may not happen right now. You may not get bored with Pokémon for a long time, but sooner or later you will. And it's nice to know that there are other games out there to play.

Another good thing about Pokémon and the Game Boy is that it just goes to show you that you don't need a bunch of fighting, punching, kicking, and skull-juggling to be a fun game. That's important to remember. Violent video games are not always the most fun. Actually, I don't like the violent games that much. And I'm not just saying that because I'm old or anything. Pokémon is a thinking game, and there's something new at every level. You have to pay attention to play it. Plus, even if you never even come close to finishing it, there's still a lot of fun stuff to do and see in it.

Another Pokémon Book

DOES THE WORLD REALLY, REALLY NEED another Pokémon book? Heck, yes! And I'll tell you why. First off, I wanted to make this book different from all the other books out there. I wanted to make it as fun as the game itself.

Is that possible? Can a book be as fun as a video game? I think so. I think books can be even more fun than a video game. And remember, books don't need batteries.

One way I thought to make the book fun, while including as much information as possible, was to have kids—actual real live kids—write a large part of the book. I can tell you the moves, the tricks, the mini–walk-throughs, and all the rest of that stuff. All of that stuff is easy. But I wanted to get kids' comments on the games, the Poké-mon, and the strategies.

Kids notice things in a game that adults might miss. Also, certain moves that may be easy for adults may be harder for kids. And last, I wanted the book to be like talking to a friend, like sharing secrets of the game in the schoolyard. I hope this book will be easier than the information in the schoolyard because it is written down, so you don't have to remember every little detail.

Another way I wanted to make this book fun was to put in a lot of stupid jokes. I read a lot of the video game books out there, and most of them are very serious. Too serious, if you ask me. You did ask me, didn't you? Okay, even if you didn't ask me, I'm telling you anyway. They're too serious! I want this book to be fun!

I did include a bunch of tips, suggestions, and hints to help you get through the really tough spots. Of course, I want people to finish the game, but even more important, I want them to have fun playing it. I also want them to laugh at some of the stupid jokes in this book. With any luck at all, this book will help you to enjoy Pokémon even more and maybe even make you laugh.

And just to show you that I'm serious about making you laugh, here's an absolutely useless Pokémon joke.

Question:

What's the difference between Pokémon and a bathroom?

Answer:

If you don't know, then you can't borrow my Game Boy!

Made you laugh, didn't I? Good. Now stop laughing and start reading. There may be more laughs, but I'm not going to tell you where they are!

I hope you like the book. And I want to thank all of the kids who contributed to it. I know they worked really hard on getting their sections done. It wasn't easy, believe me. They did it in their free time, after they had finished their homework and chores.

They took the time to write about their favorite game because we can all learn something from each other. No matter how young someone is, he or she can still show us some cool things. And that goes for practically everything, not just for Pokémon.

Two of the kids who offered a lot—I mean *a lot*—of help are Max S. and Willy S. of Brooklyn, New York. So you'll see a lot of their comments throughout the book. They love Pokémon and play it all the time—sometime even when they're supposed to be doing homework. Since Max and Willy are twins, they have a real advantage over other kids. They always have someone around to play the game and trade Pokémon tips with. Both of them have collected all 150 Pokémon, so that makes them experts. They were also really enthusiastic about sharing what they learned with other kids.

Another kid who really helped out a lot was Tim R. from New Jersey. He did a really great job of writing up all his favorite Pokémon stuff. But when the book was almost done, he called again and said his favorite city had changed. So Tim's favorite place in the game is now the Unknown Dungeon. I think that's pretty cool because Tim had been playing the game a long time and was still discovering stuff and having a great time doing it.

A bunch of other kids who helped out include Michael D., Aaron R., and Raymond K. from New Jersey and Colin J. from Brooklyn, New York. They did great jobs too. Naturally, other kids also helped out, but they didn't make it into the book. I'd like to thank them too. Thanks, guys.

Will This Book Make Me a Better Pokémon Player?

I CAN ANSWER THAT QUESTION IN ONE word. Nope! The only thing that can make you a better Pokémon player is playing Pokémon. Hey, no book can make you a better player. Books can tell you how to finish the game, but finishing the game doesn't mean you are a better player. It just means someone told you how to finish the game. What's the fun in that?

What I tried to do is include a bunch of stuff that will help you understand the game. And a bunch of tips and hints that will help you over the tough spots. That way, if and when you do finish the game, you did it on your own without me telling you how to go every inch of the way.

Remember, the whole idea behind Pokémon isn't to finish the game quickly but to have fun playing it. Even if you never finish the game to its end, you can still have loads of fun collecting, trading, and battling with friends.

What's All That Stuff in the Back of the Book? This is a Pokémon Book!

RELAX! CHILL OUT AND CALM DOWN! I included a whole bunch of other Game Boy games in the back of the book for fun. And yes, I know this is a Pokémon book. It says so right on the cover. On the other hand, sooner or later you may want to play a different game. Look at it this way: What if you just had to eat ice cream forever? How much fun would that be? Okay, bad example. It probably would be a lot of fun.

Let's look at it another way. Suppose you bought the Game Boy just to play Pokémon. Finally, you've done all the collecting and trading and had all the adventures you ever wanted to have. By this time you're maybe 120 years old. You put your Game Boy and Pokémon cartridge down and say, "Stupid game! That was easy. It only took me 110 years to beat it! And it needs batteries again! What a rip-off! Stupid game!" You look around and what do you see? You see this book! And suddenly you realize that you can play other games on the Game Boy! Plus, a lot of the games are the same ones you used to play on your television. But you haven't played the console since your parents grounded you for life when you were 97 years old because of that little incident with the goldfish and your big sister. Now, finally, you can try out all those other cool games for the Game Boy.

That's the kind of stuff I was thinking when I included the information for the other games. You may not appreciate them now. But just wait 100 years or so, and you'll really enjoy those games.

Pokémon: The Game
(for Parents and Kids)

POKÉMON BEGAN IN JAPAN A LITTLE OVER three years ago. And today it's still a favorite with Japanese kids. As a matter of fact, while there are only two cartridges available in the United States, with two more coming, in Japan they have more game cartridges to choose from. Today Pokémon is one of the hottest-selling video games in the world. Among the facts cited is that Pokémon cartridges are selling at the rate of about 10,000 a day.

What is probably most amazing about this is that it's for the Nintendo Game Boy, a system that is a decade old. As I told you before, in the world of computer games, ten years is ancient technological history.

Pokémon doesn't have the fancy-pants

graphics or the super-difficult, fast game play. Above all, it doesn't have the violence currently found in many video games. While there is fighting in the Pokémon game, the object of the game is not to kill the monsters you encounter but rather to capture, train, and collect them.

For many Americans, the first time they heard the word "Pokémon" was in news stories about an unfortunate incident in which several hundred children were reportedly adversely affected by the flashing multicolored display used in a cartoon sequence in Japan. That sequence was removed before the cartoon was broadcast in America.

Today Pokémon games are just one piece of a vast Poké Empire that includes not only the television show, but toys, clothing, trading cards, and events held in shopping malls. One cold-cuts manufacturer even came out with Pokémon products.

Pokémon has cut to the heart of what kids want in a video game. Fancy graphics, violence, and negative themes were not what captured the imagination of kids. Neither was it an ocean of products related to the game, including a television show. It was solid and imaginative game-play.

Why This Game Is Cool (Parents, Are You Reading This?)

THE PLOT OF POKÉMON REVOLVES AROUND a young boy named Ash Ketchum (as in "Catch 'em") and his adventure to capture and train all 150 Pokémon included in the game. The game is a very basic role-playing game (called RPG) very similar to console-type video games, such as Zelda or Super Mario. The young hero of the story—Ash—explores his imaginary world searching out Pokémon. Once he finds one, he uses his tame Pokémon and a Poké Ball to capture them. He then goes about training and "evolving" the Pokémon.

Pokémon is, in fact, not a fighting game but an exploring and collecting game. Young players are encouraged not to hurt the wild Pokémon but to care for them.

They are also encouraged to "trade" Pokémon. By connecting a cable link between
two hand-held games, kids can trade electronic characters. These trades can be either
temporary or permanent, depending on the
conditions the children set between themselves. The kids also may trade between the
two versions (red and blue). Trading is encouraged within the game rules, with
traded characters gaining skills more
quickly.

Is Pokémon good or bad? Like any other
video game or television show, too much of
a good thing is always bad. It is the parents'
responsibility to monitor all forms of entertainment their kids consume, whether it is
television, movies, books, magazines, or
video games. And it is up to the kids to trust
their parents' judgment and obey the rules.

Warning:
This Could Happen to You!

HOW IMPORTANT IS POKÉMON? IT DEPENDS
on how much you like playing the game.

For a lot of kids it's a game to play once in a while. For other kids it's a game to play all the time. It may even be their favorite game of all time. However, no matter how much you like Pokémon, no matter how good you are at playing Pokémon, and no matter how much you want to play Pokémon, remember: *It is still only a video game*. It's not as important as doing your chores around the house. And above all, it's not as important as school or homework. No question about it! No question at all.

School and homework are more important. But some kids, it seems, didn't quite understand that or got too excited. Schools around the country are starting to ban Pokémon! They are banning Pokémon Game Boys, cards, and even clothing. Why? Because the kids were paying more attention to Pokémon than to their schoolwork, and some of the kids were losing their Game Boys, cartridges, or cards. What a mess! So, the teachers and principals got together and made a rule: NO MORE POKÉMON!

Think about it. You wouldn't bring your

television from home to watch your favorite show in class. You wouldn't ask a teacher to teach history in a video arcade. So, why make a problem with Pokémon in school?

There are a lot of other reasons why Pokémon doesn't belong in school. For one thing, it's a hard game to play and you'll make mistakes if you're not giving it your full attention. Besides, if you're rushed or distracted, you won't even enjoy it that much. And you might lose it altogether on the playground or on the way home.

So keep school for learning and not for Pokémon.

Pop Quiz!

Question: When are video games more important than schoolwork?

A. Always.

B. Only when I'm winning.

C. I can't read this; I spend too much time playing video games.

D. Never.

Correct Answer: D. I know you were hoping for another answer, but there just isn't one. Video games, even great ones like Pokémon, are never more important than schoolwork.

Pokémon Glossary

THERE'S A LOT TO KNOW ABOUT POKÉMON. Everyone forgets something sometimes. So, here's a handy and dandy glossary of things included in the game. Yes, I know, you probably already know all this stuff. It's "baby stuff," right? Well, as I said, everyone forgets something sometimes, so isn't it good to know this information is here if you need it?

Ash: Ash Ketchum, a young boy and the hero of the story.

Badges: You win Badges during the game play when you do something good. There are eight different Badges in the game, including the Boulder Badge, the Earth Badge, and the Rainbow Badge. You will need Badges to win the game. See the section on Badges for complete details of what powers they give you and your Pokémon Party.

Boss: Video game slang for the bad guy you have to fight. The Bosses in Pokémon are Gym Leaders, the Elite Four, and your rival.

Cable Club: Located in the Poké Center, you can go to the Cable Club either to trade Pokémon or to challenge a friend to battle. You must go to the Cable Club to trade or fight even if you are using a Color Game Boy with Infrared connection.

Cart: Short for the word "cartridge." You may also see or hear the term "game cart," which is a "game cartridge." Inside the cartridge, which goes into your Game Boy, is the software (computer language) that holds your Pokémon adventure. You wouldn't think that such a little cartridge could hold so much fun, would you? The words "cart" and "cartridge" are also used to describe "console game" software. Console games are the ones you play with a system like Nintendo 64 and hook up with your television.

Common: In Pokémon the word "Common" means that there are a lot of them. "Common" Pokémon are easy to find, and a lot of them exist in the game. Pokémon that are difficult to find, and there are very few of them, are called "Rare."

Elemental Stone: There are five different stones that Pokémon need to evolve. They are Water, Moon, Thunder, Fire, and Leaf Stones. You can simply buy them in the Celadon store or find them in Item Balls. The Moon Stone can be found in dungeons.

Elite Four: You will encounter the Elite Four near the end of the game. In fact, the Elite Four are the four biggest battle challenges of the game. They are the four trainers, Lorelei, Bruno, Agatha, and Lance. All have Pokémon with levels above 50. And each one specializes in a different type of Pokémon.

Evolve: When a Pokémon changes (grows) into another form through experience, it is said to evolve. Evolved Pokémon are stronger and better fighters. However, not every Pokémon evolves. The ones that don't evolve into anything else are rarer and more valuable.

Faint: What a Pokémon does in battle if it is not up to fighting an opponent.

FAQ: A common term used in video game books or Internet sites. FAQ stands for Frequently Asked Questions. It's pronounced like the word "facts," so it sounds like what it is.

Game Pack: (also "game pak" and just plain "pak") The game cartridge that contains the software that *is* the game. The Game Boy "reads" the information stored in the cartridge depending on what buttons you push to play the game. The words "game pack," "pack," and "pak" also are used to describe "console game" software.

Gym: Found in the cities and towns, Gyms are where you test your Pokémon against the Gym Leaders' and Pokémon Trainers'.

Gym Leaders (sometimes called Trainers):
Your major opponents in the game, they
can be found in gyms in the major cities.
There are eight Gym Leaders. When you
defeat them, they give you things, like
Badges and Technical Machines.

Health Point (also called HP): These are the
points or measurement of how healthy
your Pokémon is during the game. A
battle may deplete (use up) some HPs,
but you can usually cure your Pokémon
and get more Health Points by using a
potion.

Hidden Machine (also called HM): Like a
Technical Machine (TM) a Hidden
Machine gives your Pokémon new battle
moves. However, unlike a Technical
Machine, a Hidden Machine can be used
for as long as the game goes on. In fact,
once a Pokémon learns a Hidden
Machine skill, it has that skill forever.
There are tons of Technical Machines but
only a few Hidden Machines. Both a
Technical Machine and a Hidden Machine

have to be given to a Pokémon type that is able to use them. For example, a machine for a Grass type Pokémon will not help a Water type very much.

Level (also called LV): The amount of skill a Pokémon has gotten in battles and training. The level (or LV) of a Pokémon will give you an idea of how well it will do against an opponent. Pokémon is different than other RPG games where the word "level" refers to where you are in the game. For instance, the Third Level is the Magic Dragon's Dungeon. In Pokémon, the word "level" mostly means the strength of your Pokémon character.

Party: This is usually when a bunch of friends come over to eat cake and wear funny hats. However, a Pokémon Party usually means the group of Pokémon you've collected and are using in the game.

Poké Ball: The thing in which you capture your Pokémon. It's round and comes in different versions: the regular Poké Ball, the Great Ball, the Ultra Ball, and the Master Ball. There is also the Safari Ball, which is good only in the Safari Zone.

Pokémon: The word is Japanese and means—as if you didn't know—Pocket Monster.

Pokémon Center: Like the Poké Mart, the Poké Center is a good place for supplies . . . and more. You can find a new box at a center, plus you can heal and feed your Pokémon there. You go to the center when you want to trade Pokémon with friends. Also, you can use the computers there to store and check up on your collection of Pokémon. The Pokémon Center is one of your most valuable tools in the game. Centers are located in every city.

Poké Mart: A store where you can buy a lot of different things, such as Poké Balls, potions, antidotes, and other items you will need to complete the adventure.

Technical Machine (TM): Like a Hidden Machine (HM), a Technical Machine will

give your Pokémon new battle moves. A
Pokémon can store up to four different
skills at a time. Both Technical Machines
and Hidden Machines have to be given to
a Pokémon type that is able to use them.

Trainers: Like Gym Leaders, only not as
powerful. If you have trouble with the
Trainers, then it's a good idea to level up
with some power before facing the
Bosses.

Pokédex: A listing of all Pokémon
information available from Professor
Oak.

Potion: A potion is a medicine that can
heal a Pokémon after he has been hurt in
battle. Potions can be bought in the Poké
Marts located all around the game. Also,
potions are only one kind of medicine
that Pokémon need. All kinds of
medicines help heal injured Pokémon.
They include antidotes, burn heal, ice
heal, and others.

Power Points (PP): A measure of how
much power a Pokémon has. Moves
require Power Points. To regain Power

Points when running low, you need to go to a Poké Center.

Rare: When a Pokémon is difficult to find or can be found in only a few places, it is called "rare."

Role-Playing Game (RPG): A video game—like Pokémon—where you are the hero in a strange world. It is your job to walk around the world and solve problems, such as collecting Pokémon. It's like exploring.

Route: The places in the game that run from one area to another. Routes are like roads (or tunnels or forests) that you must travel to get from one place to another. Lots of action takes place on these routes, so when traveling you better keep alert.

Skill: The way in which your Pokémon fights in a battle. Some Pokémon skills are learned and others are natural. A Pokémon can get skills either by reaching a certain level or by use of a Technical Machine (TM) or Hidden Machine (HM).

Trading: The game feature that allows you to exchange one Pokémon character for another. Some of the trading is done in the game. However, the main trading is done with two players who both have Game Boys. A cable (sold separately) connects the two units and the players can trade Pokémon back and forth. Once you trade a Pokémon with a friend, you can trade back at any time.

Types: Pokémon come in 15 different types: Normal, Grass, Water, Fire, Poison, Dragon, Ground, Rock, Flying, Psychic, Electric, Ghost, Bug, Fighting, and Ice.

Walk-Through: Another common video game term that you'll find for other games, not just Pokémon. A walk-through is step-by-step instructions for every level of the game. Sometimes a walk-through is simply written down; other times it may contain actual maps.

Stuff You Should Know

I CALL THIS CHAPTER "STUFF YOU SHOULD KNOW." In my humble opinion, I believe that everyone should know the state capitals, the multiplication tables up to 12, and at least three good jokes. If you happen to know three jokes about state capitals and multiplication tables, then you're way ahead of everyone else. Your parents will brag about how gifted and smart you are, and teachers will allow you to get away with countless pranks.

Red and Blue

IN BETWEEN LEARNING MULTIPLICATION tables, state capitals, and jokes, you should know that Pokémon cartridges come in two colors, red and blue. In Japan, there are more colors, but right now in the United States there are just red and blue.

Both the red and blue games have the same controls on the Game Boy. They also have the same places to visit. And the plot is the same. So if you spent weeks playing the red cartridge and suddenly you're at your cousin Artemis's house and he only has the blue game, you won't have to re-learn the whole game. The red and blue versions play almost exactly the same. Only a few small things are different.

The blue version has 11 Pokémon not included in the red version. And the red version has 11 Pokémon not included in the blue version. That means in order to collect all 150 Pokémon, you have to trade with a friend. Trading is part of the game.

"Well, I like Nintendo and I liked watching the Pokémon TV show on at 7:00 A.M., so that's when I found out about Pokémon for Game Boy. I got started playing

when I got red and blue versions for Christmas in Rhode Island. I live in New Jersey. When I started playing, I started playing the blue version because I like blue more than red."

—**Tim R.**

Bonus Tip: Don't use the Poké Balls too early on in a battle. Wait until your opponent's power level is low.

Besides the fact that some different Pokémon are included in the red and blue versions, Pokémon you can buy at the Coin Exchange cost different amounts. These different prices have no effect when you play the game for a long time. In my experience, the prices all kind of equal out in the end. So you shouldn't let prices fool you into buying one color game or the other.

"When we were real little my mom and dad would dress me

and Willy different to tell which was which. I was the red twin and Willy was the blue twin. I think that's why I still like red. So, when we started playing, I was automatically the red and Willy was the blue. The two games were different when we started playing. After we began to trade, there was almost no difference."

—Max S.

Choosing Your Name and Pokémon

"Charmander, Bulbasaur, Squirtle, I didn't know which one to choose, I did eeny-meeny-mineymoe . . . and chose Squirtle. He worked out very well. When I was almost at the end of the game I had a Blastoise."

—Michael D.

"Since I can choose any name, I picked my own name. It's just easy to remember. For my rival, I always pick my teacher's name. I won't tell you why, but you can guess. When I choose a Pokémon at the beginning of the game, I almost always choose Charmander. I choose him because he can fight with fire, which is really a great strength."

—**Max S.**

"I started playing Pokémon when I received a Pocket Game Boy and the blue and red versions of the Pokémon game for Christmas. The first time I played I chose Squirtle because he is the most powerful of the three main Pokémon. Then I had to go to the Poké Mart and deliver this letter to Professor Oak from the guy in the Pokémon."

—**Raymond K.**

What to Get at the Poké Mart

ALL KINDS OF ITEMS ARE HIDDEN throughout the game. Sometimes these are difficult to get and sometimes they're really easy to find. The major items you want to get are Potions, Antidotes, and, of course, Poké Balls. These aren't everything you'll need, but they will help you and are necessary to winning the game.

> **Bonus Tip: Beware of items sold outside of Poké Marts. Often they are too expensive.**

This chapter is filled with stuff that you should know. Hey, I'm telling you priceless information here! So, listen up! Pay attention! Okay, okay, I confess. This is all stuff that I had left over and didn't know where to put it. I could have put it in the back of the book. I could have put it in the front of the book. But I put it here, so keep reading and you might learn something.

**Bonus Tip: The younger a Pokémon
is when you capture it, the better
it is to train.**

Badges

AS YOU ROAM AROUND THE GAME, THERE IS
a lot of stuff to remember. One of the most
important things to remember is to get the
Badges. You earn Badges by fighting different Leaders in the gyms. They will help you
in your quest to win the game. Now, there
are eight different kinds of Badges and each
type does something different. The Badges
play a very important role in the game if
you are serious about trading. Some Badges
will let you trade for very powerful Pokémon with very high levels, and they will
obey you. Without these Badges, Pokémon
will ignore you.

Here they are:

Boulder Badge: This is a very important
Badge because it increases your attack
strength.

Cascade Badge: When you have this Badge, Pokémon up to level 30 will obey you. Be sure you have this handy-dandy Badge before trading for powerful Pokémon.

Thunder Badge: A very cool Badge indeed, and very helpful. The Thunder Badge gives your Pokémon a speed boost.

Rainbow Badge: Like the Cascade Badge, the Rainbow Badge will give you power over more powerful Pokémon levels. With a Thunder Badge all Pokémon up to Level 50 will obey you.

Marsh Badge: With the Marsh Badge all Pokémon up to Level 70 will obey your orders.

Soul Badge: The Soul Badge increases your defensive powers, making you more difficult to attack.

Volcano Badge: The Volcano Badge increases your offensive powers, making your attacks more difficult to defend against.

Earth Badge: The Earth Badge may be the most powerful Badge of all. With the Earth Badge *all* Pokémon will obey you, no matter what their level is.

> *"You really need all of the Badges, so don't be afraid to battle the Gym guys. The Badges help you with your Pokémon and let you get the TMs. Here are where I found the Badges. I won the Boulder Badge from Brock. I won the Cascade Badge from Misty. I won the Thunder Badge from Lt. Surge. I won the Rainbow Badge from Erika. I won the Marsh Badge from Sabrina. I won the Soul Badge from Koga. I won the Volcano Badge from Blaine. And I won the Earth Badge from Giovanni."*

> —Max S.

**Bonus Tip: You cannot capture Gym
Leaders' Pokémon, so stop trying.**

Potions

POTIONS CAN BE YOUR BEST FRIENDS IN (OR
after) a battle. They help to cure injured Pokémon. There are seven different kinds of
potions, and each one does something different. They can be purchased in the Poké
Marts, though be warned, some are very
expensive and you have to spend your
money wisely. The more powerful the potion, the more it will cost you!

Potion: This regular potion cures some
"Health Points" (HPs) but not a lot. The
standard potion only replaces or heals up
to 20 HPs.

Super Potion: This potion is more powerful
and cures or heals up to 50 HPs.

Hyper Potion: This potion is even more
powerful and heals up to 200 HPs.

Full Restore Potion: Cures and heals almost everything!

Max Potion: Cures and heals everything!

Revive Potion: Works on any Pokémon that have fainted but only gives them some of their HPs back.

Max Revive Potion: Works on Pokémon that have fainted and gives all their HPs back.

Power Point (PP) Potions: Please, no jokes about PeePee Potions, I've heard them all. These PP Potions are Elixir, Max Elixir Ether, and Max Ether.

More Pokémon Medicine

Antidote: Cures Pokémon that have been poisoned.

Awakening: Cures and wakes up Pokémon that have been put to sleep.

Burn Heal: Cures Pokémon that have been burned.

Full Heal: Cures and heals just about everything, including poison, sleep, burn, freeze, and paralyzed Pokémon.

Ice Heal: Cures Pokémon that have been frozen.

Paralyz Heal: Cures Pokémon that have been paralyzed.

> *"One of the really cool things is how the drinks work. Fresh water helps a Pokémon in a fight, but soda helps him more and lemonade even more. You can buy this stuff at Celadon."*
>
> **—Willy S.**

Bonus Tip: Brush after every meal and don't eat too much candy. Will this make you a better Pokémon player? No,

**but it's hard to play when you
have a toothache!**

Repel!

REPEL SPRAY IS LIKE POKÉMON BUG SPRAY. You're going to need it to hunt wild Pokémon. Luckily, it comes in three different strengths: Repel, Super Repel, and Max Repel. Naturally, you can buy these at any Poké Mart. Repel sprays keep the wild Pokémon away from your weaker Pokémon, but only for a little while. Often a little while is all you need to save your Pokémon. The Repel sprays are different strengths, as I mentioned, but they don't work for any longer amount of time, only for greater distances.

Vitamins!

JUST LIKE YOU, THE POKÉMON IN YOUR party should remember to take their vitamins. Actually, you should remember to feed them their vitamins. You'll be glad you did when you take them into battle. Most of the vitamins can be found in the Celadon Department Store or in item balls hidden away in dungeons. But wherever you find them, remember that they contain important powers that your Pokémon need in battle!

Protein: A great boost for attacks.

Calcium: Increases each Pokémon's special powers.

Iron: Boosts defense strengths. A good vitamin when going against a tough opponent.

Carbos: Increases a Pokémon's speed.

. . . And Candy Too!

"I used to use the Candy right away. That was a big mistake. It is better to save the candy and use it to raise the level of Pokémon

*when it gets harder to raise their
Level."*

—Max S.

**Bonus Tip: Soda is better for
Pokémon than water. Not like real
life, but that's the way
it is.**

Those Weird Fossils

*"I found these weird fossils in
Celadon City store and in Mt.
Moon. Most of them didn't work
until I reached Cinnabar Island.
The Scientist there knows what to
do with them."*

—Max S.

Fossils are some of the most mysterious
parts of the game. They are good for something, but not right away. You will need
them to collect all 150 Pokémon. So listen
up: *Collect those fossils and hold on to them!*

"There were fossils and an amber stone that works like a fossil. I know amber isn't a stone. The fossils are Helix and Dome. They turn into Omanyte and Kabuto. Amber turns into Aerodactyl."

—Willy S.

The Real Deal Behind Skills

THERE ARE TWO WAYS TO ACQUIRE SKILLS. The first way is easy: Your Pokémon has the skill built-in from the start depending on what type it is. But the Pokémon can get other skills by gaining Technical Machines and Hidden Machines. Also, they get new skills by evolving to new and higher levels. That's another reason why it's good to evolve: You gain more skills.

However, not even Pokémon can do everything. Each Pokémon can only keep up to four different Skills. This is very important to remember, because if you have a Pokémon with four skills and want to teach it something new, then it's going to have to "forget" something. You are going to have to make a choice about which skill is more important to you and your strategy.

> *"I used to try to make my Poké-*
> *mon have just one kind of skill,*
> *like all attack types. That didn't*
> *work out very good with some of*
> *the harder Gym Leaders. I have*
> *them learn attack and defend*
> *skills now, and they do better*
> *battling Gym Leaders."*
>
> **—Max S.**

Bonus Tip: Remember when a Pokémon learns a move on its own, it is more powerful than learning it with a TM. TMs are best used to teach moves that a Pokémon can't learn on its own.

Money!

IT'S TRUE THAT MONEY CAN'T BUY HAPPI-
ness, but it can buy some pretty neat stuff in
the stores you'll find in Pokémon. In fact,
you need money and lots of it to win the
game. Hey, those Ice Heal potions don't
grow on trees!

So how do you go about getting money?
There are two main ways to get money. The
first way is to fight a Trainer or Leader and
win. After you beat the Trainer or Leader,
then you'll receive a "reward." The second
way to get money is to use the Pay Day
move. The way to get Pay Day is to capture
Meowth and raise it to Level 17. You can
also get Pay Day with TM#16.

*"I was worried about running
out of money after I beat the
Trainers. But if you beat all the
Trainers then you can still get
money by fighting the Elite Four.*

Beating the Elite Four is worth a whole lot of money."

—Willy S.

Bonus Tip: Whenever you find or get a Nugget, sell it! Nuggets are worth 5,000 in Poké Marts!

Ten Pokémon Questions Answered

Question 1:
What is a Pikachu, and where can I find one?

Answer:
Pikachu is one of the rare Pokémon and a real favorite among players. It is #25 in the list. It's an Electric type, which means it's good when going against Water and Flying types. However, even though it's cute, it's still hard to find. In fact, there are only two places in the game where you can find them: the Viridian Forest and the Power Plant.

Question 2:

I finished the game and still
don't have every Pokémon.
What do I do now?

Answer:

That's okay. You've really done
something just by finishing.
When the game is over you will
be returned automatically to
Pallet Town. There you can
wander around and collect all
the Pokémon you missed your
first time through, including
Mewtwo, who is back at the
Secret Dungeon.

Question 3:

I have a new Color Game Boy.
Do I have to use the electric eye
to play a friend in the Cable
Club?

Answer:

No, you don't have to use the infrared connection. You can use a cable, too. As a matter of fact, some players prefer the cable when playing in places like cars or in the schoolyard.

Question 4:

How long should it take to finish the game?

Answer:

That's really, really hard to say. Some people have walk-through guide books and can finish the game in several hours. However, if you are like me, then you believe that they are not really playing the game. They are just following directions. That's not to say that I totally hate walk-throughs. Sometimes they can be good, if you get stuck someplace and need some help. But back to the question: Playing the game without a guide can take anywhere from 50 to 100 hours! Wow! That's a long time! But remember, Pokémon isn't a game that counts how long you take to finish it. So, think of it as a lot of game for your money.

Question 5:

I traded a Pokémon with a friend at the Cable Club, and now I want to trade it back. But my friend says that it's impossible. Is he right?

Answer:

No, your friend is wrong. You can trade your Pokémon back.

Question 6:

Some of the stuff on some of the levels doesn't work. I can't get into some places. Plus, in Cerulean City a bike was 1,000,000! I'll never get enough for that.

Answer:

That's one of the most valuable lessons you can learn in a role-playing game. Good role-playing games (RPGs) don't go from start to finish with one level or place after another until the end. Sometimes you have to go back to a place you were already at in order to get something you need. For instance, later on in the game you'll get a Bike Voucher and have to return to the Cerulean City bike store. The trick is remembering where that bike shop was in the first place. So don't feel bad about going back to a place you already visited to get something or do something. It's all part of the game!

Question 7:
Who or what is MISSINGNO? Is it the 151st Pokémon?

Answer:
No, MISSINGNO is a computer programming mistake. It's been turning up around Cinnabar Island and its number is 000. When it's caught, it doesn't add to your Pokédex. Also, I've heard from those who should know that saving the game after you catch it can distort the game you have saved. So you should definitely not try to save or trade it.

Question 8:

Is there one super Pokémon type?

Answer:

No, but there is a Super Pokémon Party. The idea is to collect a well-balanced party that includes all the different types of Pokémon and raise them to the highest levels you can. That way you'll be ready for the Gym Leaders.

Question 9:

Is there a trick to winning the game fast?

Answer:

No, and if there was, then it probably wouldn't be a very good game. Pokémon is about

enjoying the adventure,
exploring, and collecting. If you
could cheat the game, you
would only be cheating yourself
of all the fun of playing it.

Question 10:

What is Pokémon about?

Answer:

Pokémon is a video game for
fun, so it really isn't about
anything except having fun.
However, you do a lot of things
in Pokémon. You collect
creatures, battle opponents, raise
your creatures to be healthy,
buy things, and explore places.
You also trade your Pokémon
with friends and battle them
through the Cable Club. A lot of
these activities, like collecting,
trading, and exploring, are all
things kids have been doing for

years. Kids love doing stuff like that! Maybe that's why Pokémon is so popular. If you want your parents or grandparents to understand Pokémon, then ask them what they collected or where they explored, then show them how you do it on the Game Boy.

Ten Stupidest Questions Ever Asked About Pokémon Answered

Question 1:
Are we there yet?

Answer:
No, first you have to play the game to get there.

Question 2:
Why don't Pokémon ever have to go to the bathroom?

Answer:
How do you know they don't?

Question 3:

I keep pushing the buttons and nothing happens.

Answer:

You have to turn the game on to play it.

Question 4:

If I collect all 150 Pokémon, can I be Boss of you?

Answer:

No.

Question 5:

Are we there yet?

Answer:

No.

Question 6:

Why did Golbat eat my homework?

Answer:

Golbat didn't eat your homework. Nice try, though.

Question 7:

Who would win if Abaham Lincoln and Geodude got into a fight?

Answer:

Nobody would win. Abraham Lincoln was the 16th president of the United States and died in 1865. Geodude is #74 Rock-type Pokémon and a character in a video game.

Question 8:

Are we almost there?

Answer:

No. I'll tell you when we get there.

Question 9:

My big brother said that if I collect all 150 Pokémon, I get a hundred billion dollars and a ride in the space shuttle. Is he lying to me?

Answer:

Yes. And the next time he brings his girlfriend over, you should show her the baby pictures of him in diapers.

Question 10:

I got carsick and threw up on my Game Boy. Did I hurt my Pokémon?

Answer:

No, they're just video game characters. But you probably didn't help your Game Boy very much.

Question 11:

Are we there yet?

Answer:

Sorry, you were only allowed to ask ten questions.

Getting the Best Pokémon

THERE REALLY IS NO "BEST" OR "WORST" Pokémon. It's like saying that vanilla tastes better than chocolate. For one thing, if you are serious about the game, then you want to collect all 150 Pokémon, anyway.

The best Trainers know their Pokémons' strengths and weaknesses and plan their strategy that way. There are, as you probably know, 15 different types of Pokémon: Normal, Grass, Water, Fire, Poison, Dragon, Ground, Rock, Flying, Psychic, Electric, Ghost, Bug, Fighting, and Ice. How you use them along the way will determine how well you play the game.

When you started building your Pokémon Party, you have to be careful to build a good all-around Party. For example, Flying and Fire Pokémon types may be your favorites. That's good. Everyone has favorite types. However, in order to win the game, you should make sure that you have a lot of different types of Pokémon, not just your favorites. All the guides say that you should pay attention to all different types equally and try to evolve them equally. I know, that's really hard. My advice is to be aware that you may have favorites and make a special effort to find, capture, and evolve even the Pokémon you don't care about. A Pokémon you didn't like at the beginning may turn into a favorite once you play and evolve it a little bit.

> *"You have to know what Poké-
> mon to use and when. That is
> really important. I start with
> Normal and Grass types. I'll tell
> you why. The Normal types are
> good fighters and help a lot at the
> beginning. When I first started
> playing, Normal types were easy
> to learn. But after I played with*

*them for a while, I didn't like
them that much in the game.
They weren't that helpful later
on. The Grass types were good
all the way through the game. I
also like the fighting guys, especially Primeape."*

—Willy S.

*"Poison types are fun, but they
are weak. Water Pokémon are
also good. I suggest Blastoise,
which is very good when you're
fighting Fire, Rock, and Ground
opponents. I also like Dragon
types, which are good and strong.
The other Pokémon I like are Flying, Psychic, and Ghost types.
These guys are really good in the
middle of the game."*

—Max S.

*"I like Pikachu because it was the
first Pokémon I ever knew. I also*

like Squirtle because in the Game
Boy it is the powerfulest of the
three Pokémon in Professor
Oak's lab and I think Squirtle is
the best of the three Pokémon in
Prof. Oak's lab. So I chose Squirtle. I like Charmander because it
has a flame on its tail, and I like
Ekans because it's a snake and I
like snakes. Bulbasaur is one of
my favorites because it has a
plant on its back. I LOVE Ditto
because it can turn into anything.
Altogether, I like Pikachu, Squirtle, Charmander, Bulbasaur, Ekans, Ditto, Gengar, Raichu,
Blastoise, Arbok, Vaporeon, and
Weepinbell."

—Tim R.

"Squirtle is my favorite character
because he is the Water-type Pokémon and he's powerful. My favorite level for the Pokémon is

1-50 because it's the most highest. I discovered that Squirtle has a Hydro pump and evolves into a powerful Pokémon."

—**Raymond K.**

"My favorite Pokémon is Mewtwo because he's the strongest Pokémon. My favorite level is 16 because that's when some Pokémon evolve!"

—**Aaron R.**

Catching Pokémon

YOU MIGHT ALREADY KNOW ALL THIS stuff, but suppose there's someone out there who doesn't know it. This section is for them. Also, if your parents ever ask about the game, then you can show them this section. And if a space alien happens to land in your backyard and asks about the game you're playing, this section might come in handy. You can tell him it's a great game played by a lot of Earth kids and then show him this section. After he reads it, tell him it is a traditional Earth welcome for him to mow the lawn and clean out the cat's litter box.

The way you capture Pokémon is with Poké Balls. Naturally. Now, you just can't whip out a Poké Ball on the critter and start training it. *Naw, that would be too easy.* What you have to do is hunt wild Pokémon and fight them first.

Where this game differs from a lot of other video games is that the idea isn't to completely beat up the Wild Pokémon you find. The idea is to tire them out so that their energy levels get low enough to capture them with the Poké Balls. This is really a great idea on the part of the guys who thought the game up. Why is this a great idea? Glad you asked. This is a great idea because, face it, the standard kicking, punching, fighting games get boring after a while. Pokémon is a game with real strategy.

For example, what if you send your ab-solute biggest, strongest guys against a

Wild Pokémon? Well, chances are they will defeat it and that will be that—no capture. So, you want to match the fighters you send against Wild Pokémon with the Wild Pokémon's strength. That way they will tire it out and you can use a Poké Ball.

> *"I was really worried about catching my first Pokémon, but I did. It just took some practice. Then I worried about Poké Balls and how they would work later on, but then I found out about Ultra Balls, for catching the really strong guys."*
>
> **—Willy S.**

Bonus Tip: Create Pokémon Parties with different types. You will need different types to finish the game.

Where's the Best Place to Find Wild Pokémon?

THESE WILD AND CRAZY GUYS ARE ALL over the place! It's true, there are dozens of places to capture Pokémon. However, for now, for someone just starting out, the best places to catch them are in the grass or in caves. Later on you can find them in forests and dungeons. But the one sure place is in tall grass. Later on you'll see Pokémon with Trainers. And you might think to yourself, "Hey, why run around in the long grass or hunting through caves? Why not just capture a Trainer's Pokémon?" Well, it won't work. Trust me. You'll probably try it anyway, so just let me say now, I told you so!

> **Bonus Tip: Wild Pokémon usually can be found in long, tall grass. Two other spots for hunting Wild Pokémon are dungeons and water.**

Hey, I Got One! I Got One!

THE FIRST THING TO DO AFTER CAPTURING your first Pokémon is to run around yelling "I got one! I got one! Yip-yip-yip-peee!" Doing this has absolutely no effect on the game, but it's fun.

The next thing you want to do is take your Pokémon to the Pokémon Center. Once there, it can get healed and will be as good as new. Then you can check out the Pokédex to find out all about it. Once you've done this, then you start training.

> *"I was kinda upset that I captured only beginner-level Pokémon when I first started playing. Then I found out that the Pokémon with lower levels learn moves faster. So that was all right."*
>
> **—Max S.**

"I captured six Pokémon and all my slots filled up. I was worried until I found out that after you fill up the slots, your Pokémon are stored in the computer at the Pokémon Center."

—Willy S.

Bonus Tip: Match Poké Balls to an opponent's strength. Don't use a ball that is not strong enough or too strong.

Evolving, Leveling Up, and Elemental Stones

"I spent a lot of time trying to evolve all of my monsters by Leveling Up with Experience. It was a waste. Now I know that you should only Level Up a few of the ones that you like best. Then you can evolve the others with Elemental Stones or by trading. The other thing to do is find one that is already evolved and capture it. All these things are easier than Leveling Up the old-fashioned way."

—Max S.

**Bonus Tip: To stop the evolving
process push the B button.**

Pokémon need different stones to evolve:
Water, Moon, Thunder, Fire, and Leaf
Stones. You can simply buy them in the
Celadon store or find them in Item Balls.
Of all the stones, the Moon Stone is the
hardest to find. Usually you can find one
in dungeons.

> *"It's pretty easy to figure out
> what Stone changes what type of
> Pokémon. The Fire Stone changes
> certain Fire types. The Thunder
> Stone changes certain Electric
> types. And the Water Stones
> change certain Water types. The
> Leaf Stones evolve the Grass
> types. It is real easy to figure out
> which goes with which."*
>
> **—Willy S.**

> *"I never use the Stones as soon as
> I find them anymore. This is why.*

*You have to wait until a Poké-
mon can no longer do any new
moves to evolve it. If you evolve
it too soon, it may never learn
any more moves or it may take
longer to learn the moves. Both
ways, it's a real pain. So when
your Pokémon can no longer
learn anything is the time to
evolve it."*

—Max S.

**Bonus Tip: Wait until your
Pokémon is trained to a high level
before using an Elemental Stone to
evolve it. Some Pokémon take
longer to learn skills once they
are evolved.**

Battle Strategies

Bonus Tip: Save before all battles.

The fighting part of the game is one of the
best parts. And it can be the most fun.

However, it also the part where you really have to know what you're doing. After all, it's no fun losing the fights that you get into, right?

One of the first tricks that any good player learns in battle is to switch your Pokémon in the middle of a fight. There's nothing wrong with this, and it's definitely not cheating. As a matter of fact, this is a great way to gain strength for weak Pokémon.

It works like this. Suppose you have a Pokémon that has a low, low Level. Choose it as your first Pokémon. Then go out and pick a fight with the strongest opponent you can find. Start fighting and then quickly switch to your strongest Pokémon. After you defeat your opponent, both your strong and your weak Pokémon will gain Experience Points. If you do this enough times, you can really build up the weaker Pokémon in your party. This method works really, really well with a weak Pokémon that you received in a trade, because it gets one and a half the number of experience points.

> **Bonus Tip: If your Pokémon is zapped by poison or a paralyzer in battle, don't restore it while the battle is still going on. It will only make it an easy target for opponents. Opponents won't go after a Pokémon that is down from poison or paralyzed.**

"My favorite Pokémon combinations for battle are Blastoise and Drowzee. I chose them because Blastoise has a hydropump and Drowzee has disable. Hypnosis and Water Pokémon are my best Pokémon in battles."

—Raymond K.

Carefully choose your Pokémon types to go into battle. There are a lot of combinations—too many to list here—but the Battle

Chart included with your game has all of them. You want to choose a type that has the best chance of beating the type that you are fighting. If you choose correctly, then you will be surprised at how many more battles you win, even if you didn't think you had the advantage. This is another reason to have as many different types of Pokémon as possible in your party.

> *"My favorite Pokémon combinations when I go into battle are Blastoise, Pikachu, Charmander, Bulbasaur, Ekans, and Ditto; or Blastoise, Weepinbell, Charmander, Pikachu, Bulbasaur, and Ekans. Also, if you have a Water Pokémon battling against a Rock Pokémon, you have a great advantage. Same thing if you have an Electric-type Pokémon and are battling a Water-type Pokémon, you also have a high chance of winning."*

—**Tim R.**

Bonus Tip: Once you beat Gym Leaders in battle, take the time to talk to them. They may have something valuable to offer you.

"I always save, all the time. And I always save before I go into a fight. If I get beat, then I can get alive again at the Pokémon Center. Also, if I accidentally kill a rare Pokémon I am trying to catch, then I can start over again without losing a lot of time."

—Max S.

"I've never tried this, but I heard that saving MISSINGNO can wreck your saved game. So I guess it counts as a Pokémon. People do use it to fight, but it doesn't appear in the Pokédex."

—Willy S.

"If you have a Candy in your item, and then you fight the MISS-

INGNO, *you get more than a
100. I want to try that with Master Balls.*"

—**Michael D.**

Suppose you have a weak Pokémon that
gets knocked out in a fight. You don't have
to heal it immediately. As a matter of fact,
you could be doing it a favor by not healing it right away. Once it's healed, it can
get knocked out again, and maybe by
something worse. Sometimes it is best to
wait until a battle is completely over to
start healing your Pokémon.

**Bonus Tip: A good way to earn
money is to fight the Gym Leaders.**

As you progress on your journey, you're
going to need Poké Balls, antidotes, and
potions. There's just no way around that
fact. You are going to need those things to
get anywhere in the game. And you are going to have to buy some of those things.

The best way to get money to buy them is by fighting the Leaders and Trainers that you find in the gyms.

> *"This is a really good secret tip. When you go to fight in a Gym, fight the Trainers first. The Trainers are like the big bosses, but weaker. They are really good practice for taking on the Leaders."*
>
> **—Willy S.**

> *"This is a good trick that my friend told me about. Once you defeat an opponent it is a good idea to talk to them. Sometimes they will give you things. This works really good for Team Rocket."*
>
> **—Willy S.**

Bonus Tip: Before going into battle, be sure to check out the level of the opponent. If you can't match the level,

**then run away and live to fight
another day.**

Battling Gym Leaders

THERE ARE EIGHT—COUNT 'EM, EIGHT!—
Gym Leaders. They are all tough guys.
Don't make any mistake about that and
don't feel bad if you don't beat them the
first time you got into battle against them
and their Pokémon. So that means: REMEM-
BER TO SAVE BEFORE FACING THE GYM
LEADERS! (I had to spell that BIG so you
would remember).

As tough as it is to win when fighting a
Gym Leader, it can be done. It is possible.
After all, it wouldn't be much of a game if
you couldn't win against these guys. As a
matter of fact, you have to win against them
to get the different Badges and TMs you
need to finish the game.

The Gym Leaders are Brock, Misty, Lieutenant Surge, Erika, Sabrina, Koga, Blaine,
and Giovanni. The most important thing
about battling these guys and their Poké-

mon is to remember what kind of Pokémon they train. That will tell you the kind of Pokémon you need to fight them. Your best chance for success is strategy and choosing your Pokémon wisely.

Brock: He's a guy who trains Rock types at his Gym in Pewter City. This should be easy to remember since Brock sounds a lot like Rock. Brock has the Rocks.

Misty: She trains Water types. Maybe that's why she is always wearing her bathing suit. Misty is like *mist* and always surrounded by water at her Cerulean City Gym.

Lieutenant Surge: He's a live wire who trains Electric types at his Viridian City Gym. That's easy to remember, since electricity *surges* through a wire. What isn't so easy is getting into his Gym, since he keeps the door locked. Tip: Check out the garbage cans around Lieutenant Surge's gym.

Erika: She is kind of a nature-loving Gym Leader. Her favorite types of Pokémon to train are Grass types. When you think of her, think of someone who loves nature and plants at her Celadon City Gym. There's so much to do in Celadon City that you might be tempted to avoid the Gym, but don't do that. Go to the Gym and meet Erika and her Pokémon.

Sabrina: This very tough Gym Leader lives in Saffron City, and you want to be extra careful when dealing with her and her team of Ghost and Psychic Pokémon. The Gym is filled with teleporters, and you really have to learn your way around. Sabrina and her team are kind of magical, like the teenage witch on TV. So that's a good way to remember her specialty.

Koga: He's the Gym Leader in Fuchsia City. He's a very difficult opponent because he has both Psychic and Poison types that he trains. Plus, he's very clever. So be careful! I can't think of a good way to remember his types, unless you say that Koga wears a toga while drinking a soda. Maybe a better way is to remember that Koga's types of Psychic and Poisonous Pokémon rely on cleverness—so, he's like Yoda from *Star Wars*. But did Yoda ever wear a toga while drinking a soda?

Blaine: Has his Gym on Cinnabar Island. He likes Fire-type Pokémon, and he's good at training them too. But it won't be easy to get into his Gym, since he has locked it up tight. It's easy to remember his type since "Blaine" rhymes with "flame." It also rhymes with "blame," so you can blame him for making it so tough to get into his gym.

Giovanni: He's the final Team Leader you have to go against, but he's a tough one! He's the leader of the Viridian City Gym and Team Rocket. He's so tough that he even makes you travel all the way back to Viridian City just to fight him. He and his Trainers all have the Ground types, but they are powerful! He has an easy name to remember with his specialty—Giovanni.

The beginning of his name, Gio, sounds like "Geo." And as you know, *geo* is Greek for "Earth." That's why they call it *geography*. See, who says you can't learn anything from a Pokémon book?

School Tip: You can use memory tricks like these for school too. They really work!

"There is no difference between battling a Pokémon trained in the wild and a Pokémon trained at a Gym. The same rules work. If you are battling a Water type you need to have an Electric type or a Grass type to win easy. It works that way for all Pokémon. It doesn't matter if they are Wild or Trained. You have to find out what works best on each type."

—Max S.

"A good way to win against the Gym Leaders is to have Pokémon

*with the same Levels that they
do. This is a good trick. If you
don't have a Pokémon with good
enough Levels, then go back
when you do."*

—Willy S.

**Bonus Tip: A Pokémon can
remember only four moves at a
time.**

**Bonus Tip: Remember, in Pokémon
it's always important to talk to
everyone—even the people you
just defeated in battle. You may
already know that Gym Leaders
will give you Badges for winning,
but they will also give you money
and Technical Machines too.**

Fighting Against Friends

AS YOU PROBABLY KNOW, YOU ALSO CAN
fight against friends at the Poké Center. Just

go into the Cable Club—the same one you go into to trade Pokémon—and hook up the cable with a friend. These are more like practice fights than real battles. They are just for fun. Remember, you can't switch Pokémon in the middle of a fight and you can't earn experience. So they are good for practice only.

Pokémon should be fun. But battling friends should be really just for fun. That means nobody should have their feelings hurt because they lost. Good sportsmanship should be a part of every Pokémon battle with friends.

> *"The good thing about fighting each other is that we get to practice for the Gym Leaders. That's where the Cable Club really comes in handy, if you want to check out a move or Pokémon before taking it into combat."*

> **—Max S.**

Trading

The Great 1 1/2 Trade Question: What does it mean when you trade a Pokémon and get 1 1/2 times the experience? Now, don't you wish you'd paid attention in math the day they were doing fractions and decimals? If you were too busy playing Pokémon to study fractions and decimals, it also means you were probably too busy losing at Pokémon too. So here's the math part of this book. Don't you dare groan or moan, you need to know this stuff. Knowing fractions and decimals might even help you in other ways besides winning at Pokémon.

Whether you see it written as 1 1/2 or 1.5, it means the same thing. Got it? Good. So, when you trade a Pokémon, you get the entire Pokémon experience plus another half. If Pokémon experience were pie, you would get an entire pie *plus* another half pie's worth of experience. And that's a pretty good deal, no matter how you slice it.

> *"I traded with Willy, then traded the Pokémon back to get the boost in experience. It didn't work. Later I found out that the Pokémon have to be in a new machine with a new Trainer to get the added experience quickly from trading."*

> **—Max S.**

"One of the good things about being a twin is that there is someone around to trade with—if he is in a good mood. If you want to reach the goal of all 150 Pokémon, you must trade. I found that Machop, Gastly, Abra and Geodude evolve when you trade them when they reach the next level."

—Max S.

Bonus Tip: A Pokémon that is traded and then traded back will not gain experience in the faster traded Pokémon mode with its original owner.

"Trading confused me for a long time. It also kept me from getting the most from the game. I thought that once you trade a Pokémon with someone you can't get it back. So I never traded the *guys I liked best. I was wrong. The game remembers that you captured the monster and you can trade it back. But don't trade with someone you'll never see again. I traded with someone who lived near my cousin's house and I never saw the kid again."*

—Willy S.

"Willy finished the game first. He got all 150 monsters. We had the idea that it would be good if he traded a high-level monster to me to help out in battles. It didn't work. The monster traded okay, but then it didn't fight right. Sometimes it didn't even listen to me. This is because I didn't have enough Badges. If you don't have enough Badges, the monster will ignore some of the stuff you tell it to do. The 'Badge I had, the Cascade, only went up to Level

30. *The Rainbow Badge goes higher, controls more monsters. If you have the Earth Badge, then all the monsters will think you have enough skill and listen to everything you tell them to do."*

—**Max S.**

Bonus Tip: When you find someone in the game who wants to trade, do it! You can always replace the Pokémon they want.

"My greatest trade I have ever done with anybody was the trade where I traded my Venonat for an Ekans. I also traded a Venonat for a Nidorino with my friend. One thing I learned is to capture two Pokémon that are the same and keep the one with the high levels and trade the Pokémon with the lower levels. Really trade for a Pokémon you

*care about. Another tip for trad-
ing is if you have a blue and a red
Game Boy, then trade with yourself."*

—Tim R.

Pay attention when you come across a
character in the game who wants to trade.
Even if you don't have the Pokémon the
character is looking for, you should remember where you met the character.
Then you can go back and trade with the
character when you do have the type of
Pokémon wanted. A smart player will find
these game characters, then trade with a
friend for the type of Pokémon the game
characters want. This can save you a lot of
time in the long run.

*"My friend and I traded Pikachu
for Nidoran because my friend
doesn't have that Pokémon and I
needed Pikachu so I can have all
the four main Pokémon. Then I*

traded Pikachu for an Ekans because Ekans are only in the red version and I wanted it in the blue version. Then I traded Oddish for Drowzee because my friend Justin wanted a Hypnosis Pokémon and because I needed an Oddish. I needed an Oddish because they are rare."

—Raymond K.

If by chance you have a Japanese version of Pokémon, you cannot trade with an American version. I know it isn't fair, but that's the way it is.

Bonus Tip: Even after you trade a Pokémon, you still have the credit for capturing it stored in your Pokédex.

Trading Rules

"I like mostly the trading. It's really fun. It's like you can take what you decide."

—Colin J.

Trading Pokémon with friends can be a lot of fun. Kids have always traded stuff. Baseball cards, marbles, stamps, all kinds of stuff. Pokémon is probably the first electronic game where you trade video game characters. That's also part of what makes it so much fun.

I've heard a few stories though about kids trading Pokémon for things besides other Pokémon. I've also heard a couple of stories about kids selling Pokémon characters for money. I don't think this is a great idea. I think there's a good chance that somebody can get his or her feelings hurt with this kind of stuff. So I'd like to set down a few rules for trading. They're

not really rules—more like suggestions—
though I believe they can go a long way
toward keeping the trading and game fun.
Remember, the best trades are the ones
where everyone is happy.

> **Bonus Tip: Always catch a few
> Common Pokémon and raise them
> up to a good level. That way you
> will always have something to
> trade with friends.**

1. Even before you link the games together, make sure that everyone
   knows, understands, and agrees to
   what is being traded. When both people involved don't understand exactly
   what is happening in a trade, you can
   get hurt feelings.

2. Trades do not have to be permanent—
   forever. Make sure everyone knows,
   understands, and agrees whether a
   trade is permanent or just temporary.

If it is temporary, then make sure you set a time for how long and stick by it.

3. Only trade a Pokémon for another Pokémon. Do not trade baseball cards, money, your bike, home entertainment system, or little sister or brother for Zapdos, Poliwrath, or Oddish. In the long run this can only lead to hurt feelings or worse.

4. Try to make fair trades. Don't try to rip off kids younger than yourself in very unfair trades. Also, know the value of what you are trading.

5. Don't change your mind after you make a trade. If you feel bad about trading a favorite character or think you made a mistake, then figure out a way to trade and get the character back. Or find someone else who will trade you for the same character.

Trading Tips

"*Evan, Quinn, Zack, and Joe— my friends—we all have Pokémons. Sometimes we argue about trades, sometimes I'll say I'll trade a Magmar for a different Pokémon, and they'll say we don't want a Magmar. So we have to think of something else to trade. Before I trade we talk about what we are going to trade. And if we agree on what we are going to trade, then we will trade them. Sometimes we trade and give them back a little while later.*"

—Michael D.

"*The best trade I made was a Level 21 Gyarados for a Level 43 Tauros. They traded because they needed Gyarados.*"

—Colin J.

How much is a Pokémon worth when you go to trade it with a friend? Well, that depends on a lot of things. How much do you like the particular Pokémon you are giving up in the trade? How much do you need that Pokémon you are giving up in a trade? And how much do you like or need the Pokémon you are receiving? All these things are important. And you should think about them carefully before trading. Here are some trading tips to help you make the best and smartest trades.

1. Do you really need the Pokémon you are getting in the trade or do you just like it? If you need it for a specific job or if it makes your Pokémon team more balanced, then you might want to consider trading. But think twice before trading a Pokémon you need for one that you like because it is your favorite type.

2. How rare is the Pokémon you are giving up in the trade? Does it have a

high level? Did it take you a long, long time to raise it?

3. If you are not trading for Pokémon who have reached the same level as the one you are giving up, then ask yourself: What makes this a good trade? The value of a Pokémon is not in its level alone. A Rare Pokémon at a lower level may be just as valuable to you as a Common Pokémon at a higher level. But only you can be the judge of that.

4. Know what you need to trade and why. If you have not yet collected all the Pokémon or if your Party needs a particular kind of Pokémon, then know what kinds you need. Make a list of what you need. It is always a good idea to make a list of the Pokémon you are willing to trade.

5. Don't trade just to get yourself out of one situation. If you need a Water

type to take on a Gym Leader, don't
be too quick to trade a Pokémon that
leaves your team shorthanded or un-
balanced.

Trading Red and Blue

YOU ALREADY KNOW THAT THE RED VER-
sion has 11 Pokemon not included in the
blue version and that the blue version has
11 Pokémon not included in the red version. Is this a mistake? An error?

Of course not. They probably did this so
that kids would trade. Now I understand
that in a perfect world, every kid has a best
friend with the other color cartridge. And
this best friend will automatically trade his
11 Pokémon for the other kid's 11 Pokémon without an argument or discussion. I
think about 11 kids live in this perfect
world. For all of the rest of us, each trade is
important and everybody wants to get a
good trade.

Take Max and Willy, for instance—the
two kids who helped me write this book.

They are identical twins and best friends. You would think that they traded easily and without argument with each other, right? After all, twins share everything, right? And they never argue, right?

WRONG! They argued a lot over what they were going to trade. They argued in the morning. They argued in the night. They talked about it. They screamed about it. They drove each other nuts about it. And that's normal.

And that's also why I wrote this section. You can look at it and get an idea of what you have and what you need. You can also see the kinds of trades that I suggest. Some of the rules are simple, such as an evolved Pokémon is worth more than an unevolved Pokémon. That's fair. But I also suggest you try getting "creative" in your trades. For instance, two pretty easy-to-catch Pokémon is often a fair trade for a harder-to-catch evolved Pokemon. That's fair, too.

So, before you trade, make sure you know what you are trading and be happy with the deal. Unfair trades are no fun.

Red Version Monsters

Ekans #23

EKANS IS A SNAKE, WITH THE ABILITY TO move quietly. It evolves to Arbok (Level 24). You can find Ekans in a lot of places, like Routes 4, 8, 9, 10, and 11.

Trader's Tip: I like to get Ekans when it is still young and evolve it myself. There's a reason for this. Ekans can be found in a lot of places, it is not very rare. So you can usually trade it easily. Plus, you can evolve it pretty quickly. So it's the difference between trading a character you have already evolved yourself to a higher level or trading a not-so-valuable character and growing Ekans yourself.

Arbok #24

ARBOK IS A POISON-TYPE SNAKE LIKE EKans. It can do all the things that Ekans can do because it is the final evolution of Ekans.

When you reach level 38, it can do an acid attack.

Trader's Tip: I use the same trading strategy for Arbok that I use for Ekans. Hey, they're both snake Pokémon, right? But remember, Arbok is fully evolved. If you want an Arbok, remember that it starts to get real interesting at around Level 17, when it can start biting. Since Ekans is not that difficult to evolve, I don't like to trade for Arbok usually. But if I do trade, I make sure that I don't trade anything rare, even a Pokémon that is not evolved.

Oddish #43

ODDISH IS A GRASS/POISON TYPE WITH A lot of neat abilities, like poison powder and the Stun Spore. It evolves into Gloom at Level 22.

Trader's Tip: Oddish is, well, odd. It is pretty easy to find, but does so many cool things you might be tempted to trade for something more than it's really worth. My advice to you is to try to get an Oddish that is young and evolve it yourself. However, be prepared to take some time, because Oddish evolves to Gloom and then to Vileplume. So, if you don't have the patience, you might want to consider trading two-for-one in order to get Oddish.

Gloom #44

ANOTHER GRASS/POISON TYPE MONSTER, Gloom is the evolved Oddish. He can be found on Routes 12, 13, 14, and 15.

Trader's Tip: Gloom is worth more than Oddish because he has already evolved up one level. So you might really want to consider a two-for-one trade for Gloom, but this really depends on how badly you want a partly-evolved monster. It is all a matter of how much time you want to spend evolving Oddish to Gloom. If you don't like Oddish or Gloom, but really need them, then you should probably trade more to get them.

Vileplume #45

VILEPLUME IS A FULLY EVOLVED GRASS/POI-son type monster. The bigger Vileplume's petals, the more poisonous its pollen.

Trader's Tip: Vileplume is the final evolution of Oddish and is definitely worth giving more in a trade if you really want it. But be careful and don't get carried away. Vileplume is valuable, but not so valuable that you should give away too many Pokémon to get it.

Mankey #56

MANKEY IS A FIGHTING TYPE MONSTER that is kinda, sorta like a monkey with a very quick temper. It evolves to Primeape at Level 28.

Trader's Tip: I like Mankey and might even trade an evolved Pokemon to get him in his unevolved form. Mankey can fight really well and is cool looking; so this monster is more valuable to me, personally. But don't tell anyone that, please.

Primeape #57

PRIMEAPE IS A FURIOUS FIGHTING CREATURE after it evolves from Mankey to this final form.

Trader's Tip: Primeape is the evolved form of Mankey. Mankey is so much fun to evolve that I don't think that I ever traded one. Even if you don't like the Fighting types that much (and some people don't), Primeape is still pretty valuable. I personally wouldn't trade two-for-one, but I would trade another evolved Pokémon for Primeape.

Growlithe #58

A FIRE CREATURE, GROWLITHE WILL DO ALmost anything to protect its territory. It can be found on Routes 7, 8, and Cinnabar Island in the Pokémon Mansion.

Trader's Tip: Growlithe is a Fire type

Pokémon and a lot of kids have found that he comes in real useful. Don't be fooled though, he's not all that rare, so don't trade a lot for him. Plus, since you'll be using him a lot, he'll evolve before you know it.

Arcanine #59

THIS FIRE TYPE CREATURE IS BEAUTIFUL AND runs quickly.

Trader's Tip: Arcanine, as you know, is the evolved version of Growlithe. He's a big guy, so you will probably have to trade an evolved Pokémon for him. He's worth it, but again, I like to get Pokémon and evolve them myself. So this is up to you.

Scyther #123

THIS VERY FAST FLYING BUG MOVES SO quickly that opponents may think there is more than one. Scyther can be found in the Safari Zone and the Coin Exchange.

Trader's Tip: I am not going to lie to you, Scyther is pretty cool and you might have to trade an evolved Pokémon and an unevolved Pokémon to get it. This monster's worth it, though. Again, Scyther happens to be one of my favorites.

Electabuzz #125

YOU CAN FIND THIS ELECTRIC CREATURE BY a power plant or causing a blackout in the city.

Trader's Tip: While Electabuzz is not one of my favorites, it is worth trading for, even if you have to throw in a Common type. Electabuzz proves very helpful in the later stages of the game.

Blue Version Monsters

Sandshrew #27

SANDSHREW DIGS DEEP UNDERGROUND and comes up only to find food. Look for this monster on Routes 4, 9, and 11.

Trader's Tip: Sandshrew doesn't really get all the cool moves until he reaches Level

24. So if you want to trade for a "partially evolved" Sandshrew it may be worth it.

Sandslash #28

THE FINAL EVOLUTION OF SANDSHREW, Sandslash will roll up into a ball with sharp points and roll toward an attacker or attack in the form of a ball. Look for Sandslash on Route 23.

Trader's Tip: I personally really like Sandslash. It's a cool Pokémon, and I've traded for it. However, it's worth a lot more when it gets cool moves like Furty swipes, up at the higher Level of 47. So you want to keep this in mind.

Meowth #52

One of the favorite Pokémon, Meowth is a Normal type that is fond of things that are round, like loose change. It can be found on Routes 5, 6, 7, and 8.

Trader's Tip: Meowth is a "must have" Pokémon, but you don't really need it right away. So wait until the right trade comes along.

Persian #53

A NORMAL TYPE POKÉMON, PERSIAN IS one of the toughest Pokémon to keep and train because of its unpredictable nature, just like a cat.

Trader's Tip: Persian, as you know, is the evolved form of Meowth. There's no getting around it, you need Persian. However, I would definitely trade for a Meowth and evolve to Persian, rather than trade for a Persian. That is because some people you trade with will try to get much more for a Persian than a Meowth.

Bellsprout #69

A GRASS/POISON TYPE CREATURE, BELL-sprout loves to munch on bugs and drink through its roots. Bellsprout is easy to find if you go to Routes 5, 12, 13, 14, 15, 24 or 25.

Trader's Tip: Bellsprout should be a fairly easy trade. I suggest trading a Grass type, which is very fair.

Weepinbell #70

A GRASS/POISON TYPE, WEEPINBELL evolved from Bellsprout and will evolve into Victreebel (Leaf Stone). Look for Weepinbell on Routes 12, 13, 14, and 15.

Trader's Tip: Since Weepinbell is the evolved form of Bellsprout, whoever you trade with for Weepinbell will want more for it than an unevolved Bellsprout. I never trade for an evolved Weepinbell. I prefer to trade for an unevolved version of this monster.

Victreebel #71

THE FINAL EVOLUTION FROM WEEPINBELL, Victreebel is a Grass/Poison type that lives in big communities in the jungle.

Trader's Tip: Victreebel is the final evolution of Weepinbell and Bellsprout. I suggest you start with the unevolved form and evolve this monster yourself.

Vulpix #37

A FIRE TYPE, VULPIX HAS A TAIL THAT splits in two as it gets older. It can be found on Routes 7 and 8, and in the Pokémon House on Cinnabar Island.

Trader's Tip: Vulpix is not that easy to find, so it might be worth trading at least a partly evolved Pokémon for this monster. If you want Vulpix badly, I would suggest you trade for Vulpix, rather than its evolved state, Ninetales.

Ninetales #38

THIS FIRE TYPE POKÉMON IS VERY SMART and very dangerous. Just grabbing one of those tails can result in a thousand-year curse.

Trader's Tip: Yes, I know, you just read that I suggested you trade for Vulpix before it evolves into Ninetales. I haven't changed my mind. The advice hasn't changed.

Magmar #126

THE PERFECT PLACE TO FIND MAGMAR IS the Pokémon House on Cinnabar Island.

Trader's Tip: Magmar is pretty rare, so you are going to have to trade something good for it. This is really true if it happens to be of a higher level when all of its really cool abilities kick in.

Pinsir #127

A FINAL FORM BUG TYPE, PINSIR SHOULD BE called "pincher" because of the big claws on its head that it uses to crush its opponents or toss them away. If you're looking for Pinsir, you can usually find it in the Safari Zone or the Coin Exchange.

Trader's Tip: Eeew, a bug! I would definitely trade a partly evolved Pokémon for him, but definitely not more than one.

Buy Me One, Buy Me One, Buy Me One!!!

In addition to trading, there is a way to actually buy Pokémon. If you don't already know this, then you should realize that at the Game Corner, you can go to the Coin Exchange and buy the following Pokémon. To me, the prices always seemed a bit high, but if you have enough money from playing the slot machine, looking around on the floor, and bugging the other players, then it's probably a good investment. I heard a rumor that you have a better chance of winning a lot of money if you first gather all the money from the floor and other players then play the slot machine. My friend told me that if you play the slot machine first, then gather up the money, you will lose.

Just don't spend all your money on overpriced Pokémon! You have to save at least some for later.

Red Version		Blue Version	
Abra	180	Abra	120
Clefairy	500	Clefairy	750
Nidorino	1,200	Nidorino	1,200
Dratini	2,600	Pinsir	2,000
Scyther	5,500	Dratini	4,600
Porygon	9,999	Porygon	6,500

"My favorite trade was a Pinsir for an Electabuzz. When I trade I look for Pokémon I can only find in a red version, because I have the blue version. I have both, but I don't like trading with my own games. It's more fun to trade with other people."

—Michael D.

Where to Go
and
What to do

FIRST OF ALL, THIS IS NOT A WALK-through. I hate walk-throughs. I don't like them because I think they take some of the fun out of the game. A game as good as Pokémon deserves to be explored and all the cool stuff in it should be discovered. A good video game should be an adventure with danger and surprises lurking behind every push of the button. That doesn't mean people don't need some help when they get stuck. So what I've tried to do in this chapter is include some of the best hints, tips, and suggestions. They won't tell you exactly where to go every step of the way, but they will point you in the right direction and, I hope, help you to enjoy the game more.

First of all, in Pokémon, unlike real life, you

should *always* talk to strangers. In real life talking to strangers is dangerous, probably one of the most dangerous things a kid can do. In Pokémon, talking to strangers will provide you with valuable clues to help win the game. Also, some of the odd little people in the game will trade Pokémon with you.

If you come to a place where it doesn't look like much is going on or is going to happen, that's the time to explore. Look everywhere. You'll be surprised by what you find!

Another thing you should know is that the game gets harder as you move through the different places. That's very common with video games. After all, it would be boring if they stayed the same. The first few places you go are pretty easy. In Pallet Town, Viridian City, and the connecting routes you'll learn some basic skills as well as get your first Pokémon. Then as you move through Pewter City and Mt. Moon, it starts to get harder. That's the way the game was designed, so don't get upset or give up. It's a good challenge. And the challenge in a video game is what keeps it interesting.

"My favorite item is Masterball. My favorite TMs are Surf, Fireblast, and Fisher. I like Fireblast the best, then Surf, and then Fisher."

—Michael D.

Bonus Tip: If you don't have enough slots for Pokémon, they are sent back to your computer for safekeeping. Before heading out on a serious Pokémon hunt, it's a good idea to get an empty box from the Poké Center.

Starting the Pokémon Adventure

Pallet Town

THE ONLY WAY OUT OF PALLET TOWN IS the Route 1 at the top of the screen. But don't leave too quickly. Remember to explore everything.

> *"I actually liked Pallet Town. A lot of people think it's baby stuff, and after a while it seems that way, but it was fun and I learned a lot about the game and how to play in Pallet Town. The Professor comes as soon as you leave at the top of the screen, but don't leave before exploring everything."*
>
> **—Max S.**

> *"The biggest problem I had was this little girl was in my way and she said, 'You can't get through. It's private property.' Then I went back to Professor Oak and he gave me a Pokédex. I went back to the little girl and she let me through."*
>
> **—Raymond K.**

Bonus Tip: Talk to everyone you encounter. And when someone asks you for a favor, do it.

Viridian City

YOUR JOURNEY HAS JUST BEGUN. BUT don't be so busy that you can't do a favor for your old friend, Professor Oak.

> *"The first problem I had was I could not quite understand how you get Poké Balls. That was my first biggest problem. I solved it by walking north all the way to the Viridian City mart where I bought Poke Balls. There are no Poké Balls in Pallet Town!"*
>
> **—Tim R.**

> *"The first time I played, I was too excited about getting the Poké Balls and forgot to get any potions. Big mistake. Now I al-*

*ways get potions and antidotes
whenever I can."*

—**Willy S.**

**Bonus Tip: Remember, Pikachu can
be caught only in the Power Plant
and Viridian Forest!**

Pewter City

GO NUTS AND "SHOP 'TIL YOU DROP" HERE.
There's lots to explore as well as buy. And
don't feel bad if you don't beat Brock the
first time you meet his Pokémon. He's a
tough Trainer to take on and you may have
to build up your Levels before finally beating him.

*"Pewter City is where you fight
your first Gym Leader—Brock.
Be careful. He has Geodude and
Onix. Both of them are Rock
types. If you win you get a Boulder Badge and a TM. My favor-*

ite part of Pewter City wasn't fighting Brock but the Museum."

—Willy S.

Bonus Tip: When you go into a Pokémon Center, don't forget to check out the Professor's computer. It contains valuable advice about your Pokédex.

Mount Moon

SORRY, YOU CAN TAKE ONLY ONE FOSSIL. But don't worry, you always can go back to get the other one. And be careful of "fishy deals" to be found outside of the Pokémon Center.

"The Trainers are really, really hard to beat on Mount Moon. Team Rocket guys are tough."

—Max S.

"You can catch Zubat, Paras, and other kinds of Pokémon on

Mount Moon. Be sure to look around. There are also lots of items, like potions and candy and things to get. If you battle the guard and win you get a fossil."

—Willy S.

"If you go to the right from Route 3, you will find Mount Moon. Even though it's quite dark, it's got lots of Rock Pokemon, like Onix and Geodude. You will almost always run into Zubat, a bat Pokémon. One of the most admired Pokemon in Mount Moon is Clefairy. I searched for hours and hours looking for Clefairy, yet I couldn't find him. That's because Clefairy is SO rare! I finally found a Clefairy a half-hour later. Clefairy can use doubleslap and evolves into Clefaible.

"As you leave Mount Moon, be sure you get one out of two rare fossils! You can get these special

fossils by beating the Team Rocket guy at the exit of Mount Moon. I think getting <u>C</u>lefairy from a slot machine in <u>C</u>eladon <u>C</u>ity is <u>C</u>-heating!"

—Tim R.

Bonus Tip: Don't be afraid to go backward in the game to get something or do something. The game was designed so that you have to go back to previous places at some point.

Cerulean City

IF YOU DON'T HAVE A POLIWHIRL, YOU should figure out a way to get one. That trade is a good deal and you can always use a Jynx.

"You need Pikachu to beat Gym Leader Misty's gang of Pokémon. They are mostly Water types. Go for the Trainers first to practice.

And don't feel bad that you can't afford the bike because it costs too much."

—Max S.

"The bike is so much that nobody can afford it. The thing to do is battle Misty and talk to Bill. He will give you and show you stuff that you need."

—Willy S.

"I thought the Daycare Center on Route Five was pretty good. Then I found out that Pokémon don't reach full levels there, so I stopped using it. My friends use it to put traded Pokémon there. One friend put his Magikarp there, because Magikarp can't battle well. Then he went back when it could battle better."

—Max S.

**Bonus Tip: Shop wisely when at
the Poké Mart. Buy what you'll
need for the next adventure.**

Vermillion City

THERE'S ANOTHER GREAT TRADE IN THIS town. Go for it! But don't miss your boat. You need a ticket, so you better go back to visit Bill at his house if you don't have one.

> *"Trade at Vermillion City! Get
> Farfetch'd Easy!"*
>
> **—Max S.**

> *"This is where you get to go on
> the boat. Bill should have given
> you a ticket for the boat!"*
>
> **—Willy S.**

> *"If you talk to the Pokémon Fan
> Club he will give you a ticket for
> a free bike. Then you can go back*

*and get the expensive bike from
before."*

—Max S.

**Bonus Tip: The computer at the
Pokémon Center called "Someone's
Computer" is really your computer.
Use it to store extra Pokémon and
other stuff you pick up along the
way.**

Lavender Town

DON'T MISS THE POKÉ MART IN LAVENDER
Town. There are lots of great medicines and
potions to buy. And you're going to need
them to be successful in the game. They also
have great Poké Balls, so you might as well
stock up on those too. Just don't get so busy
shopping that you forget to explore the rest
of the town.

*"You have to get to Mr. Fuji. He
will give you a Poké Flute. He
will be in the Pokémon House."*

—Max S.

Bonus Tip: If you can't get into a door or other entrance, then remember where it was and come back to it later in the game.

Celadon City

"When you go to Celadon City, there's a big department store. It just looks like a Poké Mart, but it's huge. You go into the elevator and go to the top floor. Walk up to the vending machines. It looks like a stack of books. If you have enough money you buy all three of the things. Fresh water, lemonade, and soda, and there's this little girl who says she wants something to drink. If you didn't buy the drinks, she won't say anything. But if you did buy the drinks, then she says she's thirsty. Give her a drink. Give her one and talk to her and she will give

*her a TM. Then give her another
drink and she will give you another TM. And the last time she
will give you a TM."*

—Colin J.

Don't worry if you spend a lot of time
here, Celadon City is *huge!* Plus, there is
lots to do and see here. The department
store in town is the next best thing to a
mall, and you have to explore it thor-
oughly. This is one of the biggest cities in
the game and you should take your time
exploring it. There's a lot of stuff you need
here.

*"The best thing in Celadon is the
store. You can buy everything
you need there. You can play the
slot machines there too. But I
never won. You can beat up a
Team Rocket guy who is standing
by a picture. The picture is really
a secret door! It leads to Team*

Rocket leader Giovanni. And battle with Gym Leader Erika."

—**Max S.**

"I never won anything playing the slot machines at Game Corner. I have two tips for making money there. Go up and start talking to the other people playing the slot machines and they will give you money. I got more than 40 coins talking to people. They give you the coins to go away. Also, if you go to the Game Corner you should keep pressing the A button. That way you can find a lot of coins lying on the floor. There are more on the floor than you can win, I think."

—**Willy S.**

"If you go left from Route 7 and into the biggest building to the left, then you've gone into the

*building with Eevee. When you
get there, in order to get Eevee
you must go to the back of the
mansion and go upstairs. Then
you can get Eevee.*

*"You can evolve the Eevee into
a Jolteon, Flareon or Vaporeon.
My favorite of these is Vaporeon
because it can turn into water,
and I like water. Also, Vaporeon's the most powerful. I
evolved my Eevee into a Vaporeon."*

—Tim R.

**Bonus Tip: After you get all the
money you can from the slot
machine players in the Game
Center, look on the ground around
the center by pressing A as you
walk.**

Saffron City

OH, I KNOW SAFFRON CITY SEEMS PRETTY
dinky compared to Celadon City. There's

still plenty to do here, and you'll be able to collect one of the most valuable items in the game here later on. What is it? Let's just say, you'll have a *ball* with it! But on your first visit, just explore and fight the Leaders in the two gyms in town.

> *"This is kind of a confusing place. It's big, but the first time I visited I couldn't do much. The best thing to do on a first visit is to fight the Leaders in the two gyms. Then find the little girl and give her the doll. She gives you a TM for a trade."*
>
> **—Max S.**

> *"You have to come back to Saffron later after you win at Pokémon Tower to rescue Silph Co. from the Rocket guys. After you rescue them, they will give you the Master Ball."*
>
> **—Willy S.**

Bonus Tip: If someone offers you something, even if it doesn't make sense, take it anyway. You don't know when it will come in handy!

Fuchsia City

AH, FUCHSIA CITY—GATEWAY TO SAFARI Zone and some Rare Pokémon. But don't be too eager to move on to Safari Zone. Explore all you can here and be sure to do favors for people who need them. There's no telling what they'll give you in return. And buy some Ultra Balls at the Poké Mart; you will need them!

"I never liked Fuchsia City much. There is not much to do except to get to Safari Zone. But you can get a good rod for fishing here from a man in one of the houses."

—Max S.

"Buy the stuff you need for Safari Zone. Save a lot in Safari Zone, because it is hard."

—**Willy S.**

Safari Zone

THERE'S A TON OF POKÉMON HERE. ALL you have to do is catch them. Easy, right?

"There are Rare Pokémon here, if you can catch them. That's hard."

—**Max S.**

"If you go north of Fuchsia City, you will enter the Safari Zone. The Safari Zone has Rare Poké-mon that you can't find anywhere else, like Kangaskhan and Rhy-horn. Every step you take in the Safari Zone is a step closer to

leaving 'cause every step you take is a second off your time. Instead of using Pokémon to battle, you use bait, rocks and the most special Poké Ball you can only find in the Safari Zone, the Safari Ball. Many of them are hard to catch, but you never know. You just might catch one!"

—**Tim R.**

"If you get to the house in Safari Zone, there is a man that will give you HM that will let you swim. You will also find gold teeth there for the warden. Get them too."

—**Willy S.**

Seafoam and Cinnabar Islands

ANY WAY YOU LOOK AT IT, THESE ARE tough places to get out of, so don't get discouraged! Besides, there's a ton—well, not an actual ton—of Rare Pokémon on Seafoam Island. And remember, the Rare Articuno lives here; it's the only place you will find it. So go for it! Just have enough Ultra Balls to do the job right. And once you leave Seafoam Island, Cinnabar Island will be a snap. Don't miss out on exploring and don't miss out on the lab. Be sure, to take your fossil to the Professor there.

> *"On the way to Cinnabar Island is Seafoam Island. There are lots of Rare Pokémon here. But it is a hard level."*
>
> **—Max S.**

> *"I found Articuno in Seafoam Island. But it took me a long time to catch him. Save before you start trying to catch him. It may take a long time to catch him. So save a lot."*
>
> **—Colin J.**

"You can fish in Cinnabar Island for Water Pokémon. Also, when you get to the Pokémon Mansion, use the statues to open doors. Go to the Pokémon lab too. The secret key is in the basement."

—Max S.

Indigo Plateau

THIS IS IT! YOU'RE ALMOST TO THE END OF the game! That wasn't so hard, was it? Okay, so it was hard, but you made it through fine, right? Just remember to be fully prepared with high-level Pokémon and lots of Badges and everything else before you enter Indigo Plateau. Why? Because this is the toughest level yet and the toughest Battles in the game!

"This is the hardest level. You have to fight the Elite Four and your rival—five Trainers without

healing at the Poké Center. Buy everything you can for the fight."

—Max S.

The Elite Four

"The toughest thing was beating the Elite Four. I finished the game except for getting the 150 Poké-mon. Now I am trying to do that."

—Colin J.

The Elite Four are the four biggest challenges of the game. The four trainers, Lorelei, Bruno, Agatha and Lance, all have Pokémon with levels above 50! So good luck!

Lorelei: She's a top trainer with a Water-type team. Her team includes Dewgong, Cloyster, Slowbro, Jynx, and Lapras.

Bruno: He's a Master trainer of Fighting types of Pokémon. His team includes Onix, Hitmonchan, Hitmonlee, and Machamp.

Agatha: She has Ghost-type Pokémon. Remember them? They are tough to beat. Her team is made up of Gengar, Golbat, Haunter, and Arbok.

Lance: Yikes! He has Dragon types. Gyarados, Dragonair, Aerodactyl, and Dragonite make up this tough team. Try using ice against them. Dragons hate ice.

The Final Battle!

THE FINAL BIG BATTLE OF THE GAME IS with your rival . . . you remember him, don't you? Well, guess what? He's baaaaack! Not only is he back, but all his Pokémon are at their maximum strength. Plus, he's got every type of Pokémon. Didn't I tell you to develop all different types throughout the game? Well, this is why that was so important.

What Pokémon does he have? Well, that depends on what Pokémon you chose at the beginning of the game. I know what you're thinking. If you chose differently this final battle would somehow be easy or at least easier. No such luck. No matter what Pokémon you chose, this final battle is a big one. So get ready.

> **Bonus Tip: Mewtwo is the most powerful and rarest of Pokémon. The best (and maybe only) way to capture him is with the Master Ball. And you get only one Master Ball.**

What about Those Route Things, Huh?

THE ROUTES IN THE GAME ARE LIKE PATHS or highways that connect the different areas, such as cities. Some cities have one entrance and one exit. Some cities have an entrance and more than one exit that leads to different places. The routes usually are where you will have a lot of your adventures and collect your Pokémon. Traveling

the Routes successfully will take a lot of
skill and patience.

I know, it sounds boring, right? Routes
sound boring. After all, whatever happens
on a road? You want to get to the cities with
the Gyms and Gym Leaders. You want to
go to the Poké Marts. Or maybe you want
to visit the Dungeons and the hideouts. You
don't want to spend your time on a stupid
route. Maybe you're thinking about when
you go on a trip with your parents. Not
much usually happens on the highway.
While on the highway during a family vacation, you stop for gas, go to the bathroom,
stop to take pictures, stop for lunch, go to
the bathroom again, whine and cry, stop to
ask directions, whine and cry some more,
and stop to go to the bathroom. Does that
pretty much describe it?

Well, things are different in fantasy.
Some of the greatest adventures in some of
the greatest books have taken place while
the hero was traveling. In the fairy tale
"Hansel and Gretel," for instance, the

brother and sister meet the witch while walking through the woods. In all the great knight stories, the knights meet their enemies on the road to some castle or party. And you can believe they didn't worry about going to the bathroom 20 times a day—those suits of armor were tough to take off!

Pokémon is no different. Some of your best adventures will take place on the journey between cities and towns. So be prepared for action.

> *"When I first started playing, I didn't like the routes. I was worried that I would choose the wrong one. And I just wanted to get there. The trick I learned is to explore the routes as carefully as the cities."*
>
> **—Willy S.**

> *"There are 25 routes. I took all of them to collect my 150 Pokémon. I think you have to take all*

of them to finish the game. You have to remember some of them. If something is blocking you, then remember it and go back later. You will find something good after it is unblocked. I found Hidden Machine 2 on Route 16—the girl in the house gave it to me—and used it to fly."

—Max S.

The Way I Play

IS THERE A RIGHT WAY TO PLAY POKÉMON? Is there a wrong way to play Pokémon? If you were to ask Einstein, Galileo, and Thomas Jefferson if there is a "right" or a "wrong" way to play Pokémon, they would probably answer "What? What's Pokémon?" Actually, they probably wouldn't say anything because they've all been dead for a long time.

Since Einstein, Galileo, and Thomas Jefferson aren't around to answer the question, that means you're stuck with me. Sorry, that's just the way it is.

So, is there a "right" or "wrong" way to play? The answer is easy: Absolutely not! It's a game, and the main thing is to have fun. If you're having fun playing Pokémon, then you're playing the "right" way. I know a lot of kids who never finished the game— never got to fight the Elite Four—and they don't care. They're too busy having fun trading and collecting Pokémon. I know other kids who have gotten all the way through the game and haven't collected anywhere near the 150 Pokémon. And guess what? They don't care either, they just like running around having adventures.

While there is no "right" way to play, there is kind of a "wrong" way to play. Not having fun is the wrong way to play. Unfortunately, since Pokémon can be a very tough game, it can be easy to get trapped or even feel trapped in one area. Sometimes it can be difficult to know how to move from one place to the next or know exactly what you're supposed to do to move on. It also can be hard to catch some of the Pokémon or defeat the Gym Leaders.

That's why I wrote this section. Hey, it's a tough game and everyone needs a little help now and again.

Consider this an emergency help chapter.

It's not a walk-through, but it can help you get out of some tough spots.

Pallet Town

THIS IS EASY, RIGHT? POKÉMON BEGINS LIKE almost every other role-playing game—easy!

The main thing to remember is that you learn as you go. So, big deal, right? What is there to learn in Pallet Town? The answer to that is easy: lots! There is lots and lots to learn in Pallet Town. For one thing, you learn to explore an area and buildings. You learn to talk to people—including your mom!—and you learn basic ways to move around.

Before I started playing my own Poké-mon (blue version), I never played anyone else's, so I learned a lot in Pallet Town. The most important thing I learned in Pallet Town is that it's okay to lose that first battle. I admit it, I picked Bulbasaur and got beat.

When you leave Pallet Town, of course,

there's only one way out. That's Route 1. Like Pallet Town, this is an easy Route. This is where you learn the basic moves and what to look for in a Route. It's also where I found my first Wild Pokémon on the way to Viridian City.

Now this is something you should think about: It's really important to finish these first stages by yourself. If you have someone else do them for you, like an older brother or sister, even if you have a friend help, then you won't learn what you need to complete the game. All the really simple stuff you do in Pallet Town and Route 1, you'll do again and again later on in the game, so it's really important to learn it as soon as you can.

Viridian City

THIS IS ONE OF MY FAVORITE PLACES IN THE game. Why? Because this was the first real city I got to explore. Okay, there's some stuff you have to do here to help out Professor Oak. You probably already know what it is—so you should take care of that (and don't forget to visit Gary) before returning to Viridian City. You also should think about battling some Wild Pokémon along the way. This will help you build up your level.

Once you're back in good old Viridian City, the fun begins. This is your chance to explore a real city. Heal your Pokémon. Buy stuff. Learn everything there is to know about the city and especially about the Poké Center and Poké Mart.

Why?

Because a lot of the really important stuff you need to know about the other cities (like how a Poké Center works and what you can buy at a Poké Mart) you'll learn in Viridian City.

Once I learned my way around Viridian City, the rest of the game was much easier for me. Some of the cities are bigger and weirder with a lot more stuff in them, but the stuff I learned in Viridian helped me for the rest of the game. For example, catching a low-level Pidgey on Route 1 is good practice for catching higher-level Pokémon later on.

Do you see how the game is "helping" you along, teaching you the stuff you need to know at the beginning? It's starting out easy to help you learn all the things you'll need to know later on when the game is much harder.

And another thing: Once you have Poké Balls and your Pokémon is healed up, you can go back to Route 1 and look for Wild Pokémon. This is another important lesson the game is teaching you. Never be afraid to go back to where you have already been! A lot of kids forget this, but it is real important. It is also a good lesson to remember for a lot of video games. In these games the idea isn't to get from one place to the next as fast as you can. The idea is more to solve a puzzle, and to do that you may have to visit the same place a couple of times. So keep that in mind.

Route 2

WELL, THERE'S NOT MUCH TO DO HERE FOR now, so I always move right on to Viridian Forest. And you know what happens there—Pikachu! Yes, yes, yes, Pikachu this and Pikachu that . . . well, I don't like Pikachu! Know why? Because I had a Pikachu that ate cheese sandwiches, then got carsick and threw up all over the back seat of my car! He must have eaten about 30 cheese sandwiches too. It wasn't pretty. Little guy sat there in the back and started yelling, "I'm gonna blow chunks!"

Okay, okay, I'm kidding. A Pikachu did not blow chunks in my car. It was disgusting to mention it, and I apologize. So, while you're in Viridian Forest you should probably catch one of the little guys. Just remember that I made the mistake of just hunting for Pikachu and missed a lot of the neat stuff the first time. I didn't miss the Trainers (the first time you'll battle one), but I missed the items I had to collect. Also, this is a good place to get your Pokémon levels up. So don't think Viridian Forest is just about Pikachu!

Pewter City

HERE'S WHERE THE GAME STARTS TO GET serious. You've already done everything you have to do in Pewter City, so now you have to rely on skill. You know about the Poké Center. You know about exploring, and you know about Gym Leaders. Now all you have to do is put all that experience to work.

The major thing you have to do is go up against Gym Leader Brock. And you have to do it with a Pokémon at a Level 13 or higher! I found that my Squirtle or Bulbasaur work well against his Rock types. And remember, don't forget to talk to Brock after you defeat his Pokémon in battle.

Route 3

WOW, DID I FIND A LOT OF TRAINERS HERE! The main thing to remember is to heal any Pokémon who need healing before going into Mount Moon. Also, you should probably try to catch a Jigglypuff, 'cause they are extremely rare.

Mount Moon

JUST WHEN I THOUGHT I HAD THE GAME mastered, they threw Mount Moon at me. Okay, some people don't have a problem on Mount Moon. But I had major, huge, gigantic problems. My problems had problems!

The first problem I had is that I kept getting lost. Mount Moon has more than one level, so you have to remember where you are while you're exploring. There's lots to do here, including catching a bunch of Zubat with your Pikachu. Plus, there are a lot of really tough Trainers to battle. See, I told you to heal up before going to Mount Moon.

One of the most important things to remember is to get the Pokémon fossil. It's in the dungeon. Yes, yes, I know there are two fossils, but you can have only one right now. You can come back for the other one later.

Route 4

THIS MAY BE KIND OF BORING COMPARED to Mount Moon, so consider it like a vacation. However, you can collect an Ekans (if you have a blue version) or a Sandshrew (if you have a red version).

Cerulean City

THIS IS IT—THE BIG TIME! IF YOU THOUGHT the game was easy up to now, then you're in for a surprise. This is a tough place. The first time I was here I got so confused that I almost quit playing the game. Then I realized that I should take my time. Hey, it didn't matter how long it took me to get out of this place. I just made up my mind to take as long as I needed to do it. After all, I was having a good time playing the game, even if I wasn't getting anywhere.

So here's the deal on Cerulean City. You have to do a lot of stuff here. None of it is anything you haven't done in the game before, you just have to do a lot of it and you have to do it better. For instance, you have to beat Misty, the Gym Leader. Then you have to talk to everyone you meet. And finally, you have to defeat a bunch of other trainers. All this stuff includes what you have to do on Route 24, Route 5, and Route 6 . . . *A rrrrrgggh!*

I'm not going to tell you everything you have to do and how to do it. The thing I will tell you, which I found out the hard way, is to ignore that kid in front of the cave. You need to come back to him later. He can't do you any good now. As for everything else, just take your time. Talk to everyone, including Bill. Basically you have to battle Trainers on Nugget Bridge, talk to Bill, and beat Misty's Pokémon in battle before you can leave to the next city. But there's a lot more to do, so take your time, okay?

Vermillion City

I TRADED HERE AND WASN'T SORRY. THIS IS where my knowledge of Pokémon value really came in handy! I also caught a Magikarp here with a fishing pole. However, the most important thing I found in Vermillion City was the S. S. *Anne*. Whatever you do, you have to get to the docks and on the boat. The S. S. *Anne* is a great place to collect items. Again, when you meet up with Gary in the captain's cabin, be sure to pay the captain a visit after defeating Gary Oak. The captain will give you a reward if you're nice to him.

In places like Vermillion City and Cerulean City Pokémon becomes a game of skill and patience. I discovered that by the time I reached these places, I had all the moves down but was challenged by the clever way the designers put the game together. For instance, after I defeated Gary, I didn't go back to the captain's cabin in the S. S. *Anne*. Big mistake. The captain is inside the cabin! After you defeat a Gym Leader, it's always a good idea to talk to him or her, right? Even though in other games you don't talk to people you just beat, in Pokémon you should. It's a good rule to always do everything twice, because you never know what you'll find the second time!

Route 11

SOME PEOPLE LIKE TO GO TO DIGLETT'S Cave before heading into Route 11. Me, I like to go into Route 11, even though it doesn't lead anywhere . . . now. At least I get the Item Finder. Imagine my surprise the first time I tried to get the Item Finder and discovered that I needed at least 30 Pokémon to get it! So if you have 30 of the little monsters, then go for the Item Finder.

Diglett's Cave

THIS WAS KINDA BORING FOR ME. I GOT Diglett and Dugtrio and left. When you leave you may be a little surprised to find that you are back at Route 2!. But don't panic. You are supposed to be there. Go to the houses and start trading. I discovered stuff that I needed there. Soon you'll be back on Route 9.

Is this confusing or what—from Route 2 to Route 9? Don't worry. Beat the Trainers and head to the Rock Tunnel.

Rock Tunnel

MORE TRAINERS TO FIGHT AND, AS I DIS-covered, it's really dark. You do have some-thing to light up the place, don't you? HM 5 works pretty well. Take Route 10 to Lavender Town.

Lavender Town

I DON'T KNOW ABOUT YOU, BUT I THOUGHT this was a pretty boring place. It's the gas station bathroom on the highway to the end of the game. So heal your monsters and stock up as best you can before getting on your way on Route 8. Route 8 leads to, where else? Route 7, which leads to Celadon City!

Celadon City

THE FIRST THING YOU'LL NOTICE ABOUT Celadon City is the place is *huge*! You should do all the usual stuff, like healing up your monsters, then head over to the Department Store. The best thing I learned is that it's always a good idea to trade with friends before going into Celadon City.

As, I found out, this is one place you definitely—absolutely—don't want to rush out of or through or anything. Celadon City is great. Explore everything! Play slot machines! Buy TMs! Party!

Now, here's another thing I also discovered. When I enter a place like Celadon City, I usually do better if I give it my full attention. That means I don't play the difficult levels while talking on the phone or riding around or anything. So if you're on the school bus and there are 7,000 kids screaming in your ear and one kid just dared another kid to eat something disgusting, then maybe you want to put Pokémon away for when you can play it in peace. Or you might want to discuss the game with friends or trade. Remember, there's a lot to do and think about here and you don't want to miss anything.

Saffron City

I USUALLY GO TO SAFFRON CITY NOW AND then to the Pokémon Tower back in good ol' Lavender Town.

By this stage of the game all of your opponents have very highly developed Pokémon. This means two things. It means that you should—if you haven't already—be paying attention to the levels of your Poké- mon. This is absolutely vital. It also means that you should be saving often.

Also, all of these places—Caledon, Saf- fron, and the Pokémon Tower—are all ex- ploring places as well as battle places. So you have to be real careful to look at every- thing and talk to everyone. This far into the game you should be experienced enough to know how important it is to explore and talk. The biggest mistake I made (along with a lot of other people) was to concen- trate just on the battles or collecting. Re- member: Exploring is just as important as battles!

Route 12, Route 13, Route 14, and Route 15!

HEY, YOU DID GET THE FLUTE, DIDN'T YOU? It's important because that's the only way you'll get Snorlax to move! I forgot it the first time because I didn't see what good a flute would do me. Who knew? These Routes are heavy-duty battle and collecting places, so go to it!

Fuchsia City and Safari Zone

I THINK OF FUCHSIA CITY AS A KIND OF PIT stop on the way to the Safari Zone (after defeating Koga, of course!). Again, the Safari Zone is the kind of place you want to take your time exploring. You can catch some great Pokémon here, but make sure to help the old gamekeeper. He's got a problem, and you should help him the best you can.

Route 16, Route 17, and Route 18

I KEPT LOOKING FOR STUFF TO DO HERE, but aside from capturing a few Pokémon, I didn't find all that much. Of course, you can head back to the Power Plant by way of the river. And you can pick up some TMs, but not much else.

Route 19 and Route 20

THESE ARE MAINLY COLLECTING PLACES, I found. But they lead to Seafoam and Cinnabar Islands.

Seafoam and Cinnabar Islands

I KNOW, I KNOW, I PUT THE TWO HARDEST places together. I'm not going to give you any clues on how to deal with them, and your life will be ruined forever. You will have to run off in Pokémon defeat to live in a foreign land and eat cold beans out of a can for the rest of your life.

And all because I didn't tell you to make sure you have a Pokémon who can push rocks. Oh, was that a clue I just gave you? Well, at least I didn't tell you that you can find Articuno on Seafoam Island. Oh, heck, I gave you another clue! Well, as long as you already know that much, then you might as well know that you are going to have to be very clever to work your way out of all the dungeons here.

Route 20 takes you to Cinnabar Island. It's not quite so exciting or difficult as Seafoam, but you can get your fossils reanimated here. Yippee! After you finish up at Cinnabar, you can head back to Pallet Town (hey, see ya, Mom, why not?), and then to Viridian City!

Viridian City

YOU HAVE PROBABLY BEEN WARNED, BUT I'll warn you again. Before even trying to take on Giovanni in Viridian City at the Gym, you better have some high-, high-level monsters. He's not kidding around. All his Pokémon are Levels 40 or higher!

Route 22 and Route 23

HEEEE'S BAAAACK! YES, YOU DO HAVE TO face Gary . . . again. Doesn't this guy ever learn?

Victory Road and Indigo Plateau

MORE ROCKS TO PUSH AND SOME MORE Pokémon to collect. Oh, and did I mention, you have to defeat the Elite Four when you get to Indigo Plateau?

What advice can I give you about the Elite Four? RUN!!!! RUN AWAY AS FAST AS YOU CAN! YOU CAN'T WIN! NOBODY CAN WIN! IT'S HOPELESS! HOPELESS I TELL YOU! THEY WILL TAKE OUR PIKACHU AND MAKE IT EAT BUGS! RUN! RUN!

Okay, okay, calm down. It is *not* hopeless. It's a tough thing to do but not impossible.

I discovered a few rules for taking on the Elite Four. And none of these rules involves running away and hiding. So calm down.

The first rule is to make sure you have a good variety of different types of Pokémon. That's really important. Plan your strategy carefully because you will be taking on Ice types, Fighting types, Ghost types, and Dragon types.

RUN!!!! RUN AWAY!!!!

The second thing to remember is that you will be fighting Pokémon of at least Level 50 and some are even Level 60 or more. So you need very strong monsters.

RUN!!!! RUN AWAY AND HIDE!!!!

The third rule is to have a lot of supplies ready before you face them. That means Ultra Balls, Max Repels, Full Restores . . . the whole works.

Just remember, you've beaten guys like this before in the game. You just have to plan carefully for these battles by having the right Pokémon at the right levels . . . and the right Items. Just *don't* run away.

Gary Again!

YES, HE'S BACK FOR ONE MORE TRY. AND he's got Pokémon at Level 60 or better. After the Elite Four, this guy should be a snap! You've beaten him a bunch of times and you can do it again. Be sure to check out his Pokémon, though. The trick is that his Pokémon depend on what you chose at the beginning of the game. His first three Pokémon are Pidgeot, Alakazam, and Rhydon, but the final three depend on the choices at the beginning.

He's tough, but he can be beaten. I've found that if I treat him like a member of the Elite Four, it's easier to win.

So good luck!

Poké On, Man!

"I have 96 Pokémon. I finished the game and went against the Elite Four and I have Mewtwo."

—**Michael D.**

The Game's Over and I Don't Have All the Pokémon!

HEY, CALM DOWN. HARDLY ANYONE GETS all the Pokémon by the time they finish the game. As a matter of fact, the game isn't over with the final battle. When you defeat your rival, the game will automatically save and take you back to Pallet Town. You'll still have all your Pokémon and the chance to take a nice stroll through the game.

For one thing, you can now go back to Cerulean City and enter the Dungeon. Remember that Dungeon? It was guarded by some guy by the stream. Well, the guy is gone and you can enter through the cave once you surf downstream.

There's a lot to do in the Dungeon. A lot of powerful Pokémon, including Mewtwo. You are going to need your Master Ball to capture him.

> *"I found Mewtwo in the basement first—I mean before my brother. He was in the Dungeon. Finding him isn't the hard part, capturing him is. I used the Master Ball. But you also need Ultra Balls, because there are a lot of very powerful Pokémon in the Dungeon."*
>
> **—Max S.**

Pokémon on the Internet

THE INTERNET IS LOADED WITH REALLY great Pokémon sites. There are thousands of them. Also, Nintendo has great Pokémon stuff on the net. However, whenever you are on the Internet, it's important to follow the basic safety rules. These rules are very important. As a matter of fact, you should copy them down and post them by your computer to remind you.

Good safety on the Internet is the same as good safety anywhere. You would not accept candy from strangers, so why accept computer downloads from strangers? Of course, sometimes on the Internet you do "talk" to strangers, so that's why you have to be really, really careful. People who seem "nice" on-line can turn out to be really bad. So you have to be extra careful.

1. Never, ever give anyone on the Internet any private information. That means never give them your real

name, your address, telephone number, or even the name of your school. That includes e-mail and posting it on a home page too.

2. If anyone on-line posts anything to you that makes you feel uncomfortable, tell your parents immediately.

3. Never agree to "get together" or meet anyone you met on-line.

4. Never agree to send anyone you have "met" on-line a picture of yourself.

5. Never accept any downloads or computer programs from someone you don't personally know.

6. Stay in public or open places on the net. Avoid "private" conversations via e-mail or other means.

Trading Log

WHAT'S POKÉMON WITHOUT TRADING? The answer, of course, is that it's Pokémon without trading and not as much fun as Pokémon *with* trading. For one thing, it's impossible to capture all the Pokémon without trading with a friend or two. And besides, trading with friends is fun, even if you're not trading to complete your collection. Now, if you're like me, you like trading stuff and keeping track of your trades. So here's a Trading Log to keep track of your trades with friends.

Hint: Before writing anything in your log, photocopy these pages so you can do as many trades as you like and keep track of them!

Trade #____

Date: _____
My Pokémon: _____
Type: _____
Level: _____
Traded with: _____
(Friend's Name)
Traded for: _____
Type: _____
Level: _____

Trade #____

Date: _____
My Pokémon: _____
Type: _____
Level: _____
Traded with: _____
(Friend's Name)
Traded for: _____
Type: _____
Level: _____

Trade #____

Date: _____
My Pokémon: _____
Type: _____
Level: _____
Traded with: _____
(Friend's Name)
Traded for: _____
Type: _____
Level: _____

Trade #____

Date: _____
My Pokémon: _____
Type: _____
Level: _____
Traded with: _____
(Friend's Name)
Traded for: _____
Type: _____
Level: _____

Trade #____

Date: _____
My Pokémon: _____
Type: _____
Level: _____
Traded with: _____
(Friend's Name)
Traded for: _____
Type: _____
Level: _____

Trade #____

Date: _____
My Pokémon: _____
Type: _____
Level: _____
Traded with: _____
(Friend's Name)
Traded for: _____
Type: _____
Level: _____

Trade #____

Date: _____
My Pokémon: _____
Type: _____
Level: _____
Traded with: _____
(Friend's Name)
Traded for: _____
Type: _____
Level: _____

Trade #____

Date: _____
My Pokémon: _____
Type: _____
Level: _____
Traded with: _____
(Friend's Name)
Traded for: _____
Type: _____
Level: _____

Trade #_____

Date: _____
My Pokémon: _____
Type: _____
Level: _____
Traded with: _____
(Friend's Name)
Traded for: _____
Type: _____
Level: _____

Trade #_____

Date: _____
My Pokémon: _____
Type: _____
Level: _____
Traded with: _____
(Friend's Name)
Traded for: _____
Type: _____
Level: _____

Trade #____

Date: _____
My Pokémon: _____
Type: _____
Level: _____
Traded with: _____
(Friend's Name)
Traded for: _____
Type: _____
Level: _____

Trade #____

Date: _____
My Pokémon: _____
Type: _____
Level: _____
Traded with: _____
(Friend's Name)
Traded for: _____
Type: _____
Level: _____

Trade #____

Date: _____
My Pokémon: _____
Type: _____
Level: _____
Traded with: _____
(Friend's Name)
Traded for: _____
Type: _____
Level: _____

Trade #____

Date: _____
My Pokémon: _____
Type: _____
Level: _____
Traded with: _____
(Friend's Name)
Traded for: _____
Type: _____
Level: _____

Trade #____

Date: _____
My Pokémon: _____
Type: _____
Level: _____
Traded with: _____
(Friend's Name)
Traded for: _____
Type: _____
Level: _____

Trade #____

Date: _____
My Pokémon: _____
Type: _____
Level: _____
Traded with: _____
(Friend's Name)
Traded for: _____
Type: _____
Level: _____

Pokémon Catch Log

THERE ARE ALREADY SOME LOGS OUT
there, but I wanted to make this one different. I wanted this one to really show the adventure of the game. Years ago explorers
gathered samples of plants, animals, and in-
sects and carefully entered information
about them in a log book. Since Pokémon is
kind of like exploring, I wanted to do the
same thing with this Catch Log. This way
you will have all the information written
down. Maybe you can use it to help friends
catch their Pokémon. Maybe you'll just
want to look back on it in a year or so to see
what you did. Anyway, I think it's kinda
cool to keep track of your catches, but you
don't have to if you don't want to.

Catch Log

Date: _____

Caught Pokémon: _____
(name)
Number: _____
Type: _____
Where: _____
# of Poké Balls Used: _____
Type of Balls Used: _____
Difficulty: _____

Catch Log

Date: _____

Caught Pokémon: _____
(name)
Number: _____
Type: _____
Where: _____
# of Poké Balls Used: _____
Type of Balls Used: _____
Difficulty: _____

Catch Log

Date: _____

Caught Pokémon: _____
(name)
Number: _____
Type: _____
Where: _____
# of Poké Balls Used: _____
Type of Balls Used: _____
Difficulty: _____

Catch Log

Date: _____

Caught Pokémon: _____
(name)
Number: _____
Type: _____
Where: _____
# of Poké Balls Used: _____
Type of Balls Used: _____
Difficulty: _____

Catch Log

Date: _____

Caught Pokémon: _____
(name)
Number: _____
Type: _____
Where: _____
# of Poké Balls Used: _____
Type of Balls Used: _____
Difficulty: _____

Catch Log

Date: _____

Caught Pokémon: _____
(name)
Number: _____
Type: _____
Where: _____
# of Poké Balls Used: _____
Type of Balls Used: _____
Difficulty: _____

Catch Log

Date: _____

Caught Pokémon: _____
(name)
Number: _____
Type: _____
Where: _____
# of Poké Balls Used: _____
Type of Balls Used: _____
Difficulty: _____

Catch Log

Date: _____

Caught Pokémon: _____
(name)
Number: _____
Type: _____
Where: _____
# of Poké Balls Used: _____
Type of Balls Used: _____
Difficulty: _____

Catch Log

Date: _____

Caught Pokémon: _____
(name)
Number: _____
Type: _____
Where: _____
# of Poké Balls Used: _____
Type of Balls Used: _____
Difficulty: _____

Catch Log

Date: _____

Caught Pokémon: _____
(name)
Number: _____
Type: _____
Where: _____
# of Poké Balls Used: _____
Type of Balls Used: _____
Difficulty: _____

Catch Log

Date: _____

Caught Pokémon: _____
(name)
Number: _____
Type: _____
Where: _____
# of Poké Balls Used: _____
Type of Balls Used: _____
Difficulty: _____

Catch Log

Date: _____

Caught Pokémon: _____
(name)
Number: _____
Type: _____
Where: _____
# of Poké Balls Used: _____
Type of Balls Used: _____
Difficulty: _____

Catch Log

Date: _____

Caught Pokémon: _____
(name)
Number: _____
Type: _____
Where: _____
# of Poké Balls Used: _____
Type of Balls Used: _____
Difficulty: _____

Catch Log

Date: _____

Caught Pokémon: _____
(name)
Number: _____
Type: _____
Where: _____
# of Poké Balls Used: _____
Type of Balls Used: _____
Difficulty: _____

Catch Log

Date: _____

Caught Pokémon: _____
(name)
Number: _____
Type: _____
Where: _____
# of Poké Balls Used: _____
Type of Balls Used: _____
Difficulty: _____

Catch Log

Date: _____

Caught Pokémon: _____
(name)
Number: _____
Type: _____
Where: _____
# of Poké Balls Used: _____
Type of Balls Used: _____
Difficulty: _____

Is There Life After Pokémon?

SO YOU'VE FINALLY DECIDED TO TAKE A break from Pokémon? Well, it's about time! It's also a good thing that there are hundreds and hundreds of other games to play on the Game Boy. And guess what? You can play some of them with a friend, using the cable you used to trade Pokémon. Cool, huh?

There's a couple of things you should know. First off, not all Game Boy games play on all Game Boys. For instance, if you have a regular Game Boy or Game Boy Pocket, it won't play all of the games designed for the Game Boy Color. Why? I don't know. Really, I don't know. I know everything except that. So, you have to check the package to make sure the game designed for the Game Boy Color will work on the regular Game Boy. Remember, check the package; otherwise it will be a big hassle. You'll have to take the cartridge back to the store.

However, will the games designed for the regular Game Boy and Game Boy Pocket work on the Game Boy Color? Sure, why not? But—and this is a big "but"—you won't have a full-color game. There will only be a few colors available that you can easily program into the system—which is pretty cool anyway.

So, remember, it's important to read the label on the game to see what kind of game—made for the Game Boy Color or regular Game Boy—you're getting.

The other question that a lot of video game players ask is if they can play their favorite Nintendo 64 games on a Game Boy. The answer, again, is yes and no. A lot of games come in Game Boy versions. A lot of games don't. You really have to check for yourself. On the other hand, since Game

Boy has been around a lot longer than Nintendo 64, you can find a lot of games for the Game Boy that are not for Nintendo 64.

NOTE: ALL THE GAMES INCLUDED IN THIS section carry an ERSB Rating of E for Everyone. Suitable for children age 6 years and up.

Classic Games

Frogger

Frogger is an oldie but a goodie. Your parents might have played this gem of a video game in an arcade when they were young. And yes, they had arcades back then, and yes, they were young. But probably a long time ago. Frogger is still a great game after all these years. Because the graphics were so simple when it first came out in an arcade version, this Game Boy version is almost exactly like the original in graphics.

The idea behind Frogger is simple. You have to help the friendly frog cross busy streets, lily ponds, and other dangerous places. If he doesn't land just right on the street, he could get squished. If he misses a lily pad, he can get eaten by an alligator.

Tip: Frogger starts off easy. You will think this game is a piece of cake. But it gets tougher with each level. So get jumping and give this arcade classic a try!

Pac-Man

OH, BOY, IF YOU NEVER PLAYED PAC-MAN, you have a treat coming! The game is legendary. It's historic! It's a work of art! Actually, it's a maze game. You probably know all about Pac-Man, but in case you don't, I'll tell you. Basically, you run your little Pac-Man guy—kind of like a sideways Happy Face—around the maze gobbling up dots. You get points for each dot you eat as you work through the maze.

So far, so good. But it wouldn't be much of a game if you just ran around a maze eating dots, right? To make the game more interesting, there are these ghost kind of things that can eat you if you're not fast enough to eat them first. That means, while you are munch-munch-munching on the dots in the maze, the ghost things come after you in the maze. Got it? Good. If you eat all the dots before you get eaten, then you win. Easy, right? Wrong. This is a hard game, just ask your parents!

Tip: Playing in a full screen mode is easy. You have to go to the Title Screen. Then press the left or the right button to pull up a "half" sign next to where it reads: Player 1. Now press Start. You should have full-screen playing mode.

Tetris DX ALSO CALLED TETRIS DELUXE. (*DX means Deluxe. Geesh, do I have to tell you everything?*)

Tetris is another arcade classic designed for the Game Boy. If you don't remember Tetris, the game was originally designed in the Soviet Union. If you don't remember the Soviet Union, it's what we call Russia now. Tetris is what is called a "puzzle game" because it works a lot like a puzzle. Squares fall from the top of the screen, and it's your job to move them in order at the bottom. It doesn't sound like fun, but really, it is. It's a real strategy game.

Those Game Boy players out there may remember other Tetris games for the unit, but this one was designed especially for the Game Boy Color version (but you can play it with other Game Boys). Everything, the squares and backgrounds, is brightly colored.

There are different "modes" or ways to play. You can either play a regular-type Tetris game or a timed Tetris game that lets you race against a time limit.

Tips: This code will allow you to move a falling piece back up to the top of the screen. To do this trick, you need a single piece, not a four-square piece. Hold the button and move the falling piece to the left side of the screen. When it touches the edge, start hitting the A button really fast. The piece will spin slowly but also move back up to the top of the screen. You can do this trick on the right side of the screen too. When you have a piece on the right side of the screen, move it to the edge and tap the B button while holding down Right on the control pad. The block will spin slowly and move back up the screen on the right side.

Tetris (THIS IS THE ORIGINAL ONE!)

Tetris was so popular that a whole bunch of other Tetris games came out. Tetris DX is just the latest of the Tetris family.

Tough Start: Those of you who are Tetris experts may want to start a game at a different and higher level. To do this, turn the game on and hold down the Down position on the pad. Then, when you select a starting level it won't be the one you chose, it will be a much tougher one. This is a good trick to play on someone who thinks he is a Tetris expert.

Tetris Attack (YET ANOTHER TETRIS PUZzle)

Super Hard Mode: There's no joking about this level, it's secret and it's the toughest one in the game. Are you sure you're ready for it? Okay, then, here's how to get to it. This only works for one-player mode, by the way. When you turn the game on to one-player mode and choose to play the machine, go to New Game. Then press and hold the Up button and the Select button at the same time. Without letting go of those two buttons, hit the A button. You'll find yourself in the super difficult mode!

Donkey Kong Land

WHAT'S THAT? YOU DON'T KNOW WHO OR what Donkey Kong is? I blame the schools for the lack of educated game players. Donkey Kong is only one of *the* most important video games ever made. Why? Because Mario, Luigi, and the others all got their start in Donkey Kong. If Donkey Kong never existed, then there would be no Mario. No Super Mario. No Luigi. The world as we know it would cease to exist.

Donkey Kong, like a lot of the other great video games, started out as a game in a video arcade. Then it was on the home systems, and then, well, the rest is history.

The best way to describe the Donkey Kong Land series is as a one-player action–role-playing game. Donkey and Diddy have to move through more than 30 levels to defeat their enemy in Ape City. It's fast and it's fun, and there's a lot to do and collect. If you like the Mario games for the console systems, then you'll love the Donkey Kong Land series.

Donkey Kong Land II: Diddy's Kong Quest

IN THE SECOND GAME OF THE DONKEY Kong Land series, Donkey Kong and his friends, Diddy and Trixie Kong, have to go up against Kaptain K. Rool and his henchmen, the Kremlings. Kaptain K. Rool has kidnapped Donkey Kong and is holding him for a banana ransom. His friends have to rescue him, and they have to beat the game and turn the tables on the Kaptain.

Donkey Kong Land III

IN THE THIRD GAME IN THE DONKEY KONG series, Donkey and his friends have to find a mysterious lost city. Who lost it? And how do you lose an entire city? I don't know, but they have to find it. Along the way they make new friends and discover some old enemies, like Kaptain K. Rool!

Asteroids

OH BOY, OH BOY, OH BOY . . . ASTEROIDS! How I love this game. For those of you who are not up on your video game history, this is one of the greatest games of all time. And it is also one of the first video games. Not *the* first, but pretty close. The game came out over 20 years ago in an arcade version, and it sucked up more quarters than almost any other game in history. It's just a fantastic, terrific, stupendous game.

For those of you who don't know the game, Asteroids goes like this. You control a little tiny spaceship in the middle of the vast unknown reaches of space. It's your job to shoot all the asteroids that come near you. If you don't shoot them, then they crash into your ship and the game is over.

When it first came out, this game was in black and white. I'm serious, black and white. No, really, there wasn't a color on the screen—please, stop laughing. If you

don't stop laughing, I won't even tell you
how cheesey the asteroids themselves
looked.

Now the game, converted to color, looks
great. If you play only one 20-year-old
video game this year, play this one.

Klax

THIS GAME WAS POPULAR IN THE ARCADES
around the time the first Game Boy came
out. Does that make it a classic? Yeah? No?
Maybe? Who cares? It's a fun game. The
object of this puzzle/strategy game is to ar-
range these color blocks together by color
as they come off a rolling conveyer belt.
Sounds easy? Just try playing it for a while.
You need at least three tiles together to
form a Klax, but then you can put up to five
tiles or squares, which make three Klaxes.
You also can speed up the movement by
pressing down on the Pad. Be warned: This
is a real mind-boggler and challenging
game.

More Classic Video Games You Might Like

Centipede/Millipede
Galaga/Galaxian
Ms. Pac Man
Paperboy
Space Invaders
Super Breakout

Hey, Who Likes Cartoons?

Twouble

EVER FEEL SORRY FOR SYLVESTER THE CAT? After all, he just wants a little snack. He can't help it if Tweety is the closest thing to a Happy Meal he ever sees, right? Well, here's your chance to help that "pudy tat." In this one-player role-playing game you get to chase Tweety around five levels and do everything you would want in a good role-playing game, like collect stuff and discover the game's secrets. That would be fun in it-self, but this game also includes a whole lot of other cartoon characters. And yes, Granny is included, but so are Marvin the Martian, Pepe Le Pew and Taz. And they all try to help Tweety.

The Bugs Bunny Crazy Castle and The Bugs Bunny Crazy Castle II

OH, YEAH, THIS IS WHAT I LIKE—ALL MY favorite Looney Tunes guys in a video game. Cool! I'm talking about major cartoon stars in a video game. Cartoon characters like Sylvester, Daffy, Bugs, and Wile E. Coyote. This is my kind of game.

It's a maze puzzle game where you have to rescue Bugs's love, Honey Bunny, from a Castle where Wile E. Coyote and Yosemite Sam have taken her. How big is the castle? It's plenty big, with more than 50 different mazes to find your way through. You have to collect all the carrots in each maze before moving on to the next maze.

Not only that, but as Bugs searches for Honey, the two arch-villains are searching for him. So he has to avoid them and find Honey. This is a good game. And look for Crazy Castle II, while you're at it.

Carrot Crazy

SOMEBODY'S SWIPED BUGS'S CARROTS AND he's not happy. Now he has to go around collecting all the stolen carrots. This really fun game also includes Daffy Duck, Yosemite Sam, Taz, and other Looney Tunes characters. Even Tweety is in the game, helping Bugs. There's a lot of running, jumping, and fun in this action-packed game.

Here's Some Other Cartoon Video Games You Might Like

Aladdin
A Bug's Life
Darkwing Duck
Disney's Mulan
Duck Tales 2
Jungle Book

Lion King
The Rugrats Movie
Talespin
Taz-Mania
Who Framed Roger Rabbit?

Racing Games

Wave Race

IF YOU HAVE A NINTENDO 64 SYSTEM, I don't have to tell you about Wave Race. I can tell you that now it's on Game Boy. Cool! Now you can Wave Race anywhere. Hey, now you can play everyone's favorite Jet Ski racing game while you're actually riding on Jet Skis—okay, maybe that's a little dangerous. But you can play it in the back of the family minivan.

The game plays pretty much like the N 64 version. You move up to more powerful Jet Skis as you win races. You can select between Circuit or Slalom, and the realism of the game is outstanding.

Better Handling: Touch a dolphin during a race and you get better control.

More Speed: Touching an octopus gives you a speed boost.

Racing Games You Might Like
F-1 Race
Rush 2: Extreme Racing USA (a car race game)
720° (a snowboarding game)

Now It's a Video Game!

Pokémon Pinball

So, Pokémon or pinball was never a board game. This game still has to go first in the section because you are reading a Pokémon book. Video pinball games are nothing new, but this is Pokémon Pinball! And Pokémon Pinball is new. So, if you can't get enough of the little monsters, then check out this Game Boy game and play in a whole new Pokémon world.

Battleship

EVERYONE KNOWS HOW TO PLAY BATTLE-
ship, right? This is the same Battleship game
that almost everyone has played as a board
game, but now it's adapted for a video
game. Battleship is cool in the video version
because you can either play against a friend—
with the Game Link cable—or play against
the game. There's also a bunch of very interesting features, like weapons onboard
the ships and subs and stuff like radar. Also,
there are different levels of play, so once
you beat the computer on one level, you
move on to the next—tougher—level.

The Chessmaster

BEFORE THERE WERE VIDEO GAMES, CHESS
was the best game in town. Only the fact
that there's no coin slot on a chess board
kept the chess arcades from cropping up.
According to legend, chess was invented to
show a young prince how to rule his king-

dom wisely. Originally, they tried teaching him checkers, but he kept jumping around (Get it? *Jumping*?).

Anyway, this is a great game. It's great because even if you don't know how to play, it will teach you. And if you already know how to play, it has 16 difficulty levels to choose from. So after you've learned the game and beat the computer, then you also can take on a real live person using cable link-up. And so what if you are not president of your school's Chess Club? There's also a Hints option that tells you what your next move should be when you are playing against the game's computer.

You also can save matches, to play later, or replay moves, to see what you did wrong or right during a game. In short, this cool little chess game has a lot of the very same features that those fancy-pants chess computers have and more.

Tips: Protect the king! Don't move your queen out into the game too early!

Legend of the River King

OKAY, I HAVE TO BE HONEST WITH YOU. I haven't actually played this game. I'm sitting here writing this and the game isn't out yet. But I heard about it and the game sounds really cool, so I figured I'd put it in the book. I know, I know, I should actually play the game first. But what if I waited, then didn't get a chance to include it? You might miss a great game, right? So I'm putting it in the book anyway.

This is an adventure role-playing fishing game! There's a whole story involved, where you have to catch a certain magical fish and use certain baits, and all of that. I just like the idea of a fishing game.

More Fishing Games You Might Like

Bass Fishing
Bass Hunter
In-Fisherman

Sports Games

All-Star Baseball '99

HERE'S A CHANCE TO TAKE YOUR FAVORITE big-league teams wherever you go.

This game has 30 professional teams and 750 actual players. Plus, you can play just one game or a full season, up to 162 games. For anyone into pitching strategy, there are a load of different pitches, like fastball, curve, sinker, and other cool pitches. And you get a choice of the computer helping you out in fielding or doing it on your own. This is one of the best Game Boy baseball games around.

Ken Griffey Jr.'s Slugfest

NO, THIS ISN'T A FIGHTING GAME. NOTHing is slugged here, except baseballs. This game includes the real teams and real players. You can play a full season or just a single game, and the video game baseball players included will have the real-life stats of the real-life players. How's that for realism?

International Superstar Soccer

THIS IS A VERY COOL AND REALISTIC SOCcer game. You won't find actual players, but there are 36 different countries to choose from. You can play three-, five-, or seven-minute time limits and choose between three different skill levels. There are a ton of other features, such as handicapping, which real soccer fans are certain to like.

Blades of Steel

HOCKEY, HOCKEY, HOCKEY! WAYNE Gretzky, the Great One, is no longer playing, but that doesn't mean you can't play a great hockey game. And Blades of Steel is a *great* game. As anyone who likes the N 64 version of the game knows, Blades of Steel has all the real NHL teams. You can choose from Exhibition (single game), NHL Full Season, Random Season, or Playoffs. Personally, my favorite mode is Playoffs. Plus, if you need practice, there is a practice area where you can develop your shooting. A very cool feature. Another great feature in this game is a Create A Player mode where you can pick the best features of different players. Be warned, though. This game plays very fast and may take a little practice to get the hang of it.

NBA Jam 99

YOU GET TO PLAY TWO-ON-TWO, BUT YOU can choose from 29 real-life NBA teams in this hoops. (Cool guys like us call basketball "hoops".) There are also four different modes of play. You can go for a realistic game, a super-fast game with super-fast players, Playoff mode, and a practice mode.

NBA in the Zone

THIS GAME OFFERS HOOPSTERS FIVE-ON-five playing action and realistic NBA teams. There are four different choices of playing: Exhibition, Versus, Full Season, Playoffs. This is a great game to play with a friend.

NFL Blitz

YES, ANOTHER GAME WITH REAL-LIFE teams. And this time the game is football. This game is a little hard for some players. On the other hand, this is one of the best football games around. If you're into a passing game, NFL Blitz is right for you.

Some Other Sports Games You Might Like

All-Star Baseball 2000
Fifa: Road to World Cup
Tennis
10-Pin Alley

The End of the Book . . . Almost

NOW THAT YOU KNOW ABOUT NOT ONLY Pokémon but some of the other games available for your Game Boy, be a nice guy and consider playing with members of your own family. Who knows? You might actually turn your older sister—maybe even your parents!—on to Pokémon. Maybe you should start them off slow with a rousing game of Asteroids or Tetris first.

One more suggestion. Limit the amount of time you spend playing video games— even if your room is clean, your homework done, and it seems like there's nothing else to do. There is always something else to do. Help your mom or dad out with the housework. Play with your baby brother. Go outside and throw a real ball around. Call your grandma and talk to her. Learn how to bake a cake, play an instrument, or build a bookcase. Once you've got that bookcase together, try to fill it up with books you have read. I guarantee you that you'll learn more by filling up that bookcase than by playing all the video games available in your local megastore. Honest!

GET THE HOTTEST TIPS ON WINNING TODAY'S COOLEST VIDEO GAMES

HOW TO WIN AT NINTENDO 64 GAMES
Hank Schlesinger
Discover essential expert tips to help you win
at Nintendo 64.
0-312-97087-0___$5.99 U.S.___$7.99 Can.

HOW TO WIN AT SONY PLAYSTATION GAMES
Hank Schlesinger
Learn awesome expert tips to help you
ace Sony Playstation.
0-312-97100-1___$5.99 U.S.___$7.99 Can.

HOW TO BECOME A POKÉMON MASTER
Hank Schlesinger
Master the mega-popular game of monster collecting that
has spawned a cartoon series, comic books, and hundreds
of other toys.
0-312-97256-3___$5.99 U.S.___$7.99 Can.